THE
DIGITAL
JEWELLER

Discover the 4 Step method to building a
thriving jewellery retail business in the digital economy

RYAN EDKINS

FOREWORD

By Stacey Hailes - Editor - The Professional Jeweller

They say video killed the radio star, but that's not strictly true.

In fact, video actually made radio stars more famous than ever before, as people could get to know them in a new way. And today, social media is adding to that.

It's the same for journalism; my area of expertise. While print subscriptions to consumer magazines and newspapers are dwindling, publications now have the opportunity to reach a wider audience online in new entraining and engaging ways.

A whole host of industries are having to learn what business means in a world dictated by digital – whether they like it or not.

Writers are now promoting Kindle versions of their books because they know that's where people are reading them, and TV channels are having to give viewers easy access to programmes online because people want to watch things on the go.

The digital revolution is inescapable. But it doesn't have to be daunting.

I remember when the iPhone first launched, I swore I would never replace my trusty digital camera or beloved iPod Nano. But now, just a few years later, everything is on my phone. Why? Because as much as I hate to admit it, having it all on one device makes my life easier.

That being said, I still use my digital camera on holidays because there is a time and a place for photos that are greater than my iPhone can take. And that's key because, in life and in business, people need to find the balance of what is good with how things once were, and what technology can do to improve, not remove.

I believe the jewellery industry is facing the same struggles as many other industries, but it's got a niche and a reason to thrive on the high street because the products sold in store are best purchased when they've been seen and touched.

Couples still want to experience going into a store to buy wedding and engagement rings, and if someone is looking for a gift as a self-purchase to mark a special milestone, it is way more satisfying to buy an item in a physical store while receiving an unrivalled customer experience.

That being said, jewellers cannot ignore the digital revolution. Instead they need to see online as a friend to embrace – not an enemy to avoid.

Times are hard at the moment, and every penny counts, so do you really want to spend all of your money on a digital presence? Or is it better to focus on driving sales in a physical store? Well, this is why you have picked up the right book. It's not about either or, it's about marrying the two together to boost business.

As the owner of a physical jewellery retail business, Ryan is on the right side of the battle. He is a true advocate for the jewellery industry, and has the knowledge and expertise to bring the best elements of digital and physical retail together.

The Digital Jeweller is not about trying to get jewellery retailers to spend lots_of money investing in online and digital innovations, it's about helping jewellery professionals use the technology available to them today to reduce costs, bolster business and bridge the gap between online and in store.

The whole book is a testament to the writer's success. He's been there, done that, and got the t-shirt, and now he's waving the flag for a concept that has transformed his business.

Because of this, The Digital Jeweller is not just insightful, but it's practical, and takes readers on a journey that covers every step of the way.

There are no bumps or surprises, just easy to follow information, practical advice, and relatable testimonials.

For example, The Digital Jeweller explores ways jewellery owners can implement best practices in store and empower staff to give them more time to truly concentrate on areas of the business that cannot be done by anyone else. Too many store owners in the industry are afraid to leave the shop floor in case they miss a sale, when they should feel confident everything will run smoothly while they deal with other areas.

The book also acknowledges the differences between stocking lifestyle jewellery and gifting items, and working with bridal pieces and bespoke designs. It addresses each of these areas, leaving no stone unturned, while elsewhere it gives practical advice on branding the name above the door, using social media platforms and creating effective marketing campaigns.

Don't believe the rumours. The truth is, online does not have to kill the bricks and mortar star. It's quite the opposite. If used wisely, the digital revolution can be used to enhance business in a way the previous generation of retailers could only ever dream of. The question is, are you going to allow it?

DEDICATION

I dedicate this book to my parents, Bruce and Denise Edkins.

To my father, Bruce, for teaching me to become a goldsmith, and for supporting my business journey through the ups and downs.

To my mother, Denise, for bringing me up to believe that anything is possible in this world, to dream big and aim high.

WHAT OTHERS ARE SAYING?

"Ryan has built his business knowledge of the jewellery industry from the ground up, from goldsmithing apprentice to now, successful business owner. I've witnessed Ryan's accelerated career route first hand over the last ten years and have found him an extremely intelligent and astute business person, who has always been quick to adopt new technologies and implement them in a jewellery context. This book shares his accumulated knowledge and is a perfect helping hand for those who need a bit of direction in their own established business, through to those just starting out who don't have a clue about how to be a 'digital jeweller'."

Rebecca van Rooijen - Founder and CEO
Benchpeg
www.Benchpeg.com

"The digital jeweller is essential reading for retail jewellers looking to future-proof their business"

Simon Forrester - CEO
National Association of Jewellers
www.naj.co.uk

"Ryan shares his journey from bench jeweller to digital master. This book offers you the chance to share his experience and the opportunity to embrace what you feel will transform your own business, for that is exactly what it will do."

Graham Dicks CEO
GV UK
www.gvukdesign.co.uk

"Digital products allow the retailer to offer an experience rather than just a sale. These products offer a new service and a new way to engage the customer which allows the customer participation in what they really want to purchase. This book shows the retailer is no longer limited to selling product from the case/shelf but interacting with them, helping them create their dream piece of jewelry."

Chris Burger - International Business Development
Gemvision - Stuller Inc
www.gemvision.com

"The Digital Jeweller is an essential read for any retailer trying to establish a successful online presence. This step-by-step guide offers simple, practical advice and will benefit all businesses, whether big or small."

Siobhan Holt - Deputy Editor
Retail Jeweller Magazine
www.retail-jeweller.com

"Ryan has clearly set out the road map toward a new proven business model befitting the internet age. Bricks and mortar retail outlets in High Streets across the globe are struggling to adapt to the new world. The Digital Jeweller is a road map, written clearly for jewellers to fully embrace technology."

Doug Henry - CEO & Assay Master
Birmingham Assay Office
www.theassayoffice.co.uk

"A clear direction as to what the jewellery retailer needs to do in order to change and grow - there is simply no choice but to go digital!"

Neeraj Nevatia – CSO
Sunjewels
www.sunjewels.com

"The how to business guide for independent retailers in today's competitive environment! I highly recommend this book for any retailer who is wanting to know what is to become the next normal"

Kapil Nevatia - CEO
Sunjewels
www.sunjewels.com

"The digital revolution has begun, bringing a new era for jewellery manufacturing and retail. It's time to get on board!"

Ed Hole - Head of Business Development
Weston Beamor
www.westonbeamor.co.uk

CONTENTS

Introduction 15

   You're closer than you think 18

The Digital Revolution 19

   The world has changed, and so should you 19

   A lot of what you know, no longer applies 22

   The Disruption Has Begun 24

   Will Your Business Still Exist? 26

   Consumers Will Have The Last Word 27

   The Harder You Work, The Less You Earn 29

   Now Is The Time 32

The Digital Jeweller Method 34

   Update Your Business Plan 37

   The Digital Jeweller Scorecard 38

1. Prepare 39

   Know Your Customer 40

   Where is Their Attention? 42

   Empower Your Staff 46

   Review Your Stock 54

   Reduce Overheads 60

   Embrace Technology 68

   A Common Mistake! 74

   Preparations Have Begun 78

2. Produce 79

    Curate a Digital Inventory 81

    Customisation 88

    Personalisation 94

    Custom Design 102

    Manufacturing 116

    Summary 122

3. Present 123

    Your Brand 124

    Your Website 132

    Face to Face 142

    Samples and Examples 150

    Summary 156

4. Promote 157

    Lead Generation 158

    Content Marketing 172

    Email Marketing 178

    Pay-Per-Click Advertising 184

    Summary 198

Four Simple Steps, Will You Succeed? 199

Acknowledgements 213

Resources and Next Steps 215

The Ethical Jeweller 219

Glossary 221

INTRODUCTION

The jewellery industry, like other industries, is going through a digital transformation. The internet has triggered a huge shift in consumer buying behaviour, offering a seemingly endless stream of choice for comparison. By simply searching for "engagement rings" on Google, I am served with thousands of different buying options, something unimaginable just 20 years ago.

Traditional jewellers are suffering. Most are trying their best to make ends meet while wondering how it got so hard so fast. The future does not look bright for retailers who apply the same strategies they had before the shift in consumer buying behaviour.

If you are a jewellery retailer looking to modernise and grow your business in a world dominated by the internet and social media, then this book is for you. This book will show you the four simple steps you will need to become a Digital Jeweller, and thrive in this ever-changing economy.

I've spent many years perfecting and improving the methods and frameworks I use to automate my business, and now I want to share them with you.

I started my retail business during a recession and grew it to in excess of £3 million in revenue per year in just three short years, reaping the rewards of a fully automated business. It now allows me to go on extended holidays, I have a beautiful family home and plenty of free time to enjoy with my wife and two daughters.

My journey towards becoming a Digital Jeweller began in 2000, when I started my apprenticeship to become a goldsmith. I began by learning how to create delicate pieces of fine jewellery by hand. I then spent the next six years perfecting the skill of crafting handmade fine jewellery for retail jewellers around the UK.

During this time, CAD design and 3D printing was starting to make noises within the jewellery industry, and I was instantly hooked. I decided to learn everything I could about this new process of creating jewellery from digital models, which drastically reduced the time it would take to produce a finished piece.

The reduced lead time was not the only benefit of creating jewellery from digital files. I soon realised that I could also show customers how the intended jewellery piece would look before we even started making it. In 2007, I decided to build my very first ecommerce website, populated with virtual images (renders) of the bridal jewellery designed in 3D. Starting with a small £500 budget to spend on Google AdWords, and a PayPal account to take payments, I was able to drive traffic to the website immediately, to test if it would work.

To my amazement, the website took sales in excess of £15,000 in its very first month, even though the site design was questionable to say the least! I now had the means to sell products to the public without having to purchase any stock, only having to create a piece once a sale was made. This is literally the perfect retail model, selling products that don't physically exist, only to realise them in a physical form once an order has been received.

I decided to double down on the AdWords spend and, just as expected, the sales then doubled. The more traffic I drove to the site, the greater the sales growth became. But, little did I know what was on the horizon. Not long after I discovered this game changing business model, a global recession ensued.

The recession hit in 2008. With it, I began to see a decline in demand for the custom jewellery we were making for other traditional retailers. As sales were increasing via the ecommerce website, I decided to partner with my father and open our first jewellery retail store in our local town of Rayleigh, Essex.

This was my first experience with bricks and mortar retail, but it made me realise how difficult it was for staff to price customised fine jewellery themselves. It was then that I had a profound realisation. If I could automate the analysis and pricing of digital jewellery files, then, in theory, I could automate the whole process of selling and creating a piece of fine jewellery from start to finish, thereby removing myself from the entire process.

To this day, my retail business is fully automated. So much so that, when a staff member receives an order for a piece of fine jewellery on the point of sale software, the product is manufactured automatically without further input required. Two weeks later, the finished piece arrives in store for the customer to collect, meeting the exact specification of precious metal and gems as requested by the customer, including additional personalisation.

I have dedicated the last 10 years of my life to overcome this challenge. To automate the pricing and visualisation of fine jewellery made from digital files, clicking just a few buttons on screen. My wish is to now share this knowledge and expertise with the aim of helping you become a Digital Jeweller, safe in the knowledge that your business is prepared for the future, whatever may come.

You're closer than you think

This book was written to help you identify the areas of your business that are strong, and those that need improvement. You've already done the hard work to learn your craft, create your brand and establish yourself as a professional jeweller. You have swkills and expertise that will easily translate when you become a Digital Jeweller. You don't have to reinvent yourself, you need only to apply what you know in a more modern way.

Simply apply the four steps covered in this book to a high standard and, within 12 months, you'll be able to call yourself a Digital Jeweller, and experience all the benefits that come with it. Be sure to make notes and follow the exercises when prompted. Skipping them will only delay your journey as you will miss important elements.

Apply yourself and commit to change, only then will you see improvements in your business and your lifestyle.

THE DIGITAL REVOLUTION

The world has changed, and so should you ...

I know a jeweller, a great jeweller, but he's not happy, and I know why. When he started his business, the key to becoming a successful jeweller was to curate a beautiful collection of jewellery from different suppliers, then display them in the window for all to see and admire.

Today, though, he's frustrated. He's brilliant at what he does but, now more than ever, he's having to compete with other jewellers that sell the same products. Like many other jewellers, he believes that the internet is to blame for the business downturn, and the struggles he currently faces.

When he started his business, the internet didn't exist and there was no such thing as a website. His only competition was a pawnbroker a few streets away. To drive footfall, he distributed leaflets to the local community and bought ads in the local newspaper.

His store was the go-to store in the area, where families and people of all ages went to buy special gifts for loved ones. Even recently engaged couples would return to shop for their wedding rings. He was considered a valuable member of the local community.

Although jewellers in other towns bought from the same catalogues, and stocked the same pieces of jewellery, back then, consumers had no means of comparing prices and, therefore, had no incentive to visit jewellers in other towns. They always purchased from their local store.

This was the "Golden Era" for jewellers, a period that jewellers still talk about today. A combination of high footfall, high margins and low competition meant he experienced a very profitable time for his business.

This is still his strategy today, though, as it is with most traditional jewellers. With the rise of the internet, he finds himself having to compete on price. Customers who regularly purchased jewellery from him, now rarely visit his store, opting to buy online instead, with free next day delivery from many other competitors.

To reduce overheads, he decided to take on more work himself. This was fine to start with, but he quickly realised that he was spending more time working for his business, than on it. He's now constantly trying to manage manufacturing, chase delayed orders and deal with upset customers.

Lately, he's been questioning everything.

He feels that he's working harder than ever, for little reward. The golden era has passed, and he's run out of ideas on how to make his business more profitable. He feels defeated, fed up, and is slowing losing his passion for the industry.

His story is not unique. I hear it all the time. Many jewellers are great at what they do, but they are no longer fulfilled by their business. The feeling of life being against them slowly creeps in, and future plans they once had, fade away.

If you relate to this story in some shape or form, then I am pleased you are taking the time to read this book. Before you reach the end, you'll realise that you don't have to make drastic changes to your business to succeed. The expertise and skills you possess are still in high demand today. It's only right that you should be highly paid for them.

Rather than running around working for your business, wishing you had more time, your business will work for you, and you'll have the time to concentrate on growing it. Customers will become a delight and your profit margins will increase. You'll spend less time chasing the next sale, and more time fielding inbound enquiries.

If you follow what I am about to tell you in this book, your business will transform into a leaner, stronger and more profitable business as a result. You'll feel less stressed, you'll make greater profits and you'll have more time to spend with your friends and family.

As a Digital Jeweller, you'll spend less time on the work that wears you out, and more time on the creative and curative side of the business that you love.

However, before I begin to share the actions you'll need to transform your business, you must first face up to some truths. Like it or not, the world has changed. We are living in a world that is very different to the one we were living in, just a decade ago. There are some new concepts you will need to embrace, and some old ideas you will need to let go of, and quickly.

A lot of what you know, no longer applies

Over the past 10 years, we have seen major growth in the adoption of new technology, which leverages the power of the internet to make it easier than ever to find an unlimited wealth of information and products at your fingertips. We also went through a global recession in 2008, which caused the failure of over 2,000 jewellery businesses in the USA alone in the following year.[1] At the time of writing this book in 2017, we saw the UK vote to exit the EU, and Donald Trump became president of the United States of America. Any decisions you made during the recession are now outdated.

We've witnessed a drastic shift in the economy, with a massive increase in entrepreneurship, and more individuals starting their own jewellery businesses on platforms like Etsy and EBay. Jewellery manufacturers are also selling directly to consumers as retailers themselves, a move aimed at increasing their bottom line and revenue. In a similar move, jewellery brands such as Pandora, Swarovski and Thomas Sabo have also started selling to consumers from their own websites, whilst opening stores and closing reseller accounts.

---

1   Jewellers Board of Trade USA figures 2009.

The internet has given rise to companies like Blue Nile and James Allen, and the price of certified diamonds has dropped significantly, allowing consumers to compare prices and even inspect diamonds online in high definition with a virtual loupe.

Many jewellery experts from a decade ago are scratching their heads today. It's safe to assume that your best ideas, formed just 10 years ago, are outdated. We are in the middle of a digital revolution.

So, where have all the consumers gone?

Well, the truth is, they haven't gone anywhere. The internet has simply presented a larger market of products, allowing for greater selection and easy comparison. This means that, if you are selling the same products as every jeweller in the country, your local customers can just as easily buy from any one of those other jewellers, possibly at a lower price.

The jewellery industry as we know it has changed. Unless you let go of your current thinking, it's unlikely you'll embrace the opportunities that are in front of you. At the core of who you are and what you do is a raw talent that has got you to where you are today. You just need to strip this back and create new ways to express it in a modern world, where everything is available and anything is possible.

This book will show you how to position yourself as a true Digital Jeweller, not competing on price, but growing your business and creating an army of dedicated followers.

Your expertise and talent as a jeweller are an asset in this modern world, and no one can take that away from you.

The Disruption Has Begun

The convergence of two world-changing technologies, the internet and 3D printing, has created a huge shift in consumer demand and manufacturing workflow. Physical products that were once stacked high on shelves to cater for demand are now being made to order, customised to every detail by the consumer.

Physical atoms are slowly being replaced by digital bits. Products that were once mass manufactured are being stored digitally and realised in physical form only when required. Printed catalogues are being replaced by infinite online databases of easily discoverable products.

We have moved on from a world where consumers had a narrow choice of products and store options in their local area, to being able to browse and search an unlimited array of products, from retailers and individuals around the world. The internet has sent consumer spending far and wide, diverting revenue from local traditional jewellers to online savvy retailers and individual designers who offer a unique style and following.

Seventeen years ago, I started my apprenticeship as a Master Goldsmith. I learnt to create jewellery by hand using traditional tools. It often took days to craft a single piece of jewellery. Towards the end of my apprenticeship, 3D printing was becoming a mainstream offering. I quickly realised that the ring that took me two days to make by hand, could now be created digitally within a couple of hours, then 3D printed the next day in wax, ready to cast into metal.

Traditional craftsmanship as we know it is becoming digitally integrated. It is now seen as a hybrid of two worlds. The digital craftsmen of today combine 3D modelling with the skills of a goldsmith, allowing them to manipulate the digital design to speed up workflow and improve the finish of the final piece.

Most jewellery retailers are yet to embrace the digital revolution. As a result, they are losing sales to forward-thinking competitors. Walk into any large jewellery retailer today and ask them for the price of a ring in a different metal. You'll be sent out of the store with a promise of a phone call as they'll need to "ask their supplier for a price". Even independent jewellers rely on the owner's expertise to provide a rough quote, often at the expense of their margin or the consumer's trust.

This is truly ridiculous to today's consumer; they expect more. Online, they can customise the colour of their watch band or Pandora bracelet and get an instant price, so why can't they choose the metal of a ring design and get an instant quote in store?

These are the times we live in. Millennials expect a certain level of transparency and service, which they get from other industries. If they are not happy, they'll tell the world about it. There's no better way to build trust than to offer a fully transparent pricing structure, with instant pricing online or in store.

Will Your Business Still Exist?

Jewellery shops are closing at an astonishing rate. According to the Jewellers Board of Trade USA, 2016 saw over 1,500 jewellery businesses close, the highest number of jewellery retailer closures since the 2008 recession.[2]

Gold hallmarking figures in the UK have also dropped by nearly 50% since the recession,[3] proof that consumers are buying fewer fine jewellery pieces. Instead, consumers are spending more on low-cost fashion led pieces.

Millennials are spending more on experiences and products that provide better value for less. Jewellers are struggling to keep up with the swift change in consumer demand, and their appetite for customisation and personalisation.

It's simply no longer good enough to merely sell from your supplier's catalogue, choosing pre-existing generic designs and products. As a jeweller, you must give your customer an experience they will share with their friends and post about on social media, showing off the jewellery they have just purchased.

Traditional jewellers have often been considered mysterious and intimidating places to visit, with consumers frequently being hounded whilst looking in the shop window. Some traditional jewellers to this day still lock their front doors, requiring customers to request entry using a buzzer.

---

2   Jewellers Board of Trade USA figures 2016.
3   British Hallmarking Figgures – Birmingham Assay Office.

If you compare this to the experience of shopping with a digital jeweller, whose products are accessible 24/7 online, it is easy to see why consumers are changing the way they buy. The modern day consumer now seeks a relaxed and unpressured buying environment, even when in your store.

Consumers Will Have The Last Word

In this digitally connected and social world, consumers love to talk about their experiences. The hotels they've stayed at, the restaurants they've eaten at, and the jewellery they've purchased. Consumers are literally documenting their lives and sharing it with others on social media. This pattern will only continue to develop further and become the norm as the internet becomes more integral to our daily lives.

There was a time when businesses would see an unhappy customer complain to just a few friends. Now, with the advent of social media, that complaint can reach thousands of people within seconds. Social media has given consumers the ability to shout about poor service and faulty products and, in return, businesses are able to respond openly and honestly.

There is a clear split between good being separated from the bad, and social reviews are becoming the key indicator of a business. Consumers seek social proof to determine whether they should make a purchase from the company or not.

Just take a recent example from the 9th of April 2017: a United Airlines passenger was mishandled on a flight by airline security after he refused to give up his seat to airline staff. A bystander was able to record the unfolding events on their smartphone. Within minutes of posting the video about the mistreatment, millions of people worldwide had seen the video. The company suffered serious negative press as a result, and their share price dropped significantly the day after the incident.

The most notable example in the jewellery industry is the backlash from the public when, in 1991, Gerald Ratner compared a set of earrings sold in his stores to a prawn sandwich, saying that the sandwich had a longer shelf life. This was picked up by the media and, subsequently, over £500 million was wiped from the value of the company and very nearly resulted in its collapse. If social media had been around at the time of this incident, I have no doubt that the impact of this statement would have been far worse as it would have reached a much larger audience, and very quickly.

Consumers are becoming more price conscious, using their smartphones to instantly compare prices with your competitors. I recently went to a well-known electronics store looking to purchase a TV. By simply scanning the barcode on the box with my smartphone, I was able purchase the TV from a competitor's store for 25% less, and have it delivered to me the next day.

It's crazy to think that this is even possible!

What is clear is that social media is here to stay, and the customer should be the focus of any sale. Give them an experience they will not forget, and they'll be your biggest brand ambassador. They'll be telling their network of friends and family about your business and why they should also buy from you.

The Harder You Work, The Less You Earn

Hard work doesn't always give you a competitive advantage, everyone works hard. Today's competitive advantage comes from knowing how to leverage technology to do the hard work for you. Automation is the key to serving more clients at the same time, and letting them self-serve themselves where possible.

Those who work the hardest tend to be the ones who are struggling to climb the ladder, or to even survive at all. They work so hard, they forget to put their head above the water to see where they're going.

I've seen businesses that have gone so far in one direction without stopping, they've ended up bankrupt as a result. To this day, I still see jewellers managing every stage of the manufacturing process in a bid to "save money". In doing so, they limit the amount of time they can spend acquiring and serving new clients, therefore costing themselves money as a result.

Here is an example workflow of how a typical jeweller in the London jewellery quarter would organise a product to be made:

First, they would visit a CAD modeller to create a 3D model of the design they wish to have made. They'd spend

15 minutes with the CAD modeller, and travel 15 minutes each way, to and from the office

They'd receive the 3D file by email, then forward it to a 3D printing bureau to have the wax model ready to collect in a couple of days

Once the 3D print is complete, they travel 15 minutes to collect the 3D printed model, then travel another 15 minutes to a casting company to have it cast into metal

With the casting complete the next day, they'd spend 15 minutes travelling back to the casting company to collect it and then travel 15 mins to a workshop to have the ring cleaned up, ready to set stones into it

After the mount is cleaned and assembled, they would travel 15 minutes back to the workshop to collect the mount, then travel 15 minutes to a specialist setting workshop, where the stones are set

They then travel 15 minutes to pick up the fully set mount before travelling another 15 mins to reach a polishing specialist to finish the ring

Once complete, they then travel 15 minutes to pick up the finished ring, and then travel 15 minutes back to the office

The whole process takes around two to three weeks, resulting in a finished product that is ready for the client. But all the running around, and the 15 minutes here, there and everywhere, soon adds up, so they are only able to process a limited number of orders every week.

If you've read the above and it sounds like something you're doing, to an extent, then you are limiting yourself and your income.

Now let's compare this to the Cadfolio custom design and fulfilment platform that automates the production of jewellery effortlessly:

1. Post a CAD design request online with clear instructions for the designer to create the 3D model

2. Receive the completed design via email within 48 hours, together with instant online pricing of the product

3. Press the order button for the product to be shipped within 10 working days with a hallmark, exact to the specification required

It takes less than a few minutes in total to create a custom designed product, and have it ordered for delivery within the customer's expected lead time. I have to pay slightly more to a supplier who looks after the whole job, but I still make the same profit margin by passing the cost on to the consumer. It then allows me to concentrate on acquiring and serving more customers, who, in turn, bring in more profit.

By automating the production of all fine jewellery, I considerably reduce the amount of time I spend on each order. It means that I can remove myself from this process completely, and allow my staff to manage the orders, thereby allowing my business to scale.

As this example shows, success is not achieved by creating more work for yourself, it is achieved by working smarter, and more efficiently. You can't expect things to change if you're not willing to get out of your comfort zone. You need to surround yourself with fresh ideas, new technology and experts in your field.

One of the clients I worked with redesigned his business to enable him to work four days per week. He went from being tired, overworked and burnt out, to earning more money, and having more time off with his family.

You owe it to yourself to stop working so hard, and to start living your life in a way that brings joy to yourself and your family. Your business should be an asset that generates income and works for you, not the other way around.

Now Is The Time

We are living in a time of extraordinary opportunity. At no point in history have so many people been connected, and so much opportunity created. Now is the time to take advantage of the digital revolution that is upon us, and to differentiate yourself from your competitors.

Before the advent of the internet and 3D printing, it was almost impossible to reach out to so many people with your message, and there was no way to customise products so easily. Everything was mass manufactured from a single mould, photographed and sold as a single piece or Stock Keeping Unit (SKU).

This is still true of many retailers today, though. I still see large department stores selling stunning designer rings in a single finger size, with no option to order in other sizes. This is truly a case of pot luck and a guaranteed returned purchase! Jewellery brands are still only offering their products in a limited number of ring sizes, and only in single metals. Consumers are sold what retail buyers decide to buy, therefore the choice is, and always will be, very limited.

We are entering a world where consumers can order products that are customised to every minute detail. The jewellery industry, however, is lagging behind. Online, I can order and customise suits, cars, cakes, shoes and even cutlery. So, why not a wedding ring or a necklace? The jewellery industry has been hit hard by the internet and change in consumer demand. We are at the beginning of a major shift in retail. As a jeweller, there has never been a better time to take advantage of the digital revolution.

Setting up an online store and a supply chain costs almost nothing, and, since the whole world can find you once you present products online, the possibilities are endless.

By following the Digital Jeweller method detailed in the following pages, you will understand the key principles of how to transform your business into a valuable asset, one that works to make you money.

THE DIGITAL JEWELLER METHOD

The internet has triggered a gradual shift of revenue away from traditional jewellers, towards tech savvy entrepreneurs and online retailers. Those who have built a strong presence both online and in their local area are ahead of most, but only just.

Traditional jewellers have been left wondering how it all changed so fast, and are struggling to make ends meet. They feel like they are working harder than they ever did before, and are slowly losing the passion they once had.

The real trailblazers are digital jewellers. Through embracing a digital inventory at the core of their business, they are taking advantage of assets they do not own.

It's not difficult to become a Digital Jeweller and it doesn't take years to achieve. There are just four steps you need to follow in order to thrive in the digital economy we live in today.

Step 1. Prepare – Analyse your business and take a digital first approach.

The jewellery industry is not what it once was, but one thing is certain, the future is digital. By taking the appropriate steps to safeguard your business from any future shifts in the economy, and by freeing up the cash you have tied up in unnecessary stock, your business will be able to navigate the ongoing digital revolution.

It's time to take a step back and take a long, hard look at the current state of your business, and then plan what you want it to become. By making the right changes to your business as a result, you can be confident that your business will become leaner, stronger and more profitable over time.

Step 2. Produce – Embrace a digital inventory that can be instantly priced and made on demand.

Customisation, personalisation and experiences. These are the key revenue drivers for digital jewellers. Offer consumers an interactive experience and add value to their purchase in the form of personalisation and customisation, and you'll build a life-long customer base.

Curate a set of digital products that can be customised and personalised online, as well as in store. This will give consumers a huge sense of satisfaction, whilst also putting them at ease with a fully transparent pricing structure.

Jewellery will always be a sentimental product; one which consumers prefer to touch and feel before they purchase. You just need to show them what's available in a digital environment, where they will feel comfortable making their choice.

Step 3. Present – Create remarkable digital interactions with your products and services.

Your online presence is even more important than your offline one. Shop windows only allow for a limited number of eyes to gaze at your products, but your online store is open to the world.

Your website is now your new digital shop window. It is by far the most important asset as a retailer, and should be treated as such. When visiting your website, your customers should be able to do everything they can in store, and more.

The way your present yourself online should also reflect your brand entirely. Any interaction you have with consumers via your website should be true to your values.

Step 4. Promote – Leverage digital tools to drive a steady stream of inbound enquiries with measurable results.

Digital advertising is still, by far, the most undervalued and under-leveraged tool at your disposal. Never in history have we been able to target our ideal customers, and display our products and services directly onto their screens with such precision.

Through meaningful insights and measurable results, you are able to maximise the return on your advertising spend, and continue to make improvements over time.

Using multiple advertising channels, and managing campaigns with proven techniques, it will help you drive awareness and, more importantly, sales by engaging consumers in the right place at the right time.

Update Your Business Plan

Having a strategy in business is paramount to your success, and this is as true today as it has ever been. At the centre of your business should be a digital first strategy, one that takes advantage of the digitally connected world we live in today.

It's time to take a step back and analyse every part of your business. You'll then be able to identify which areas need attention, and plan your route to success. By following the four steps I've just highlighted, and executing them to a high standard, you'll start seeing the results you have been searching for.

It is important to follow these steps in the correct order. Don't try to work solely on the one area you feel you are weak in. Jewellers often feel that digital marketing is the weaker area of their business, but they don't see the bigger problem at hand. No matter how much is spent on driving people to your business through advertising, if the model is broken, then it's wasted money. It will only further contribute towards the demise of the business.

It's time to learn the digital skills of tomorrow and start applying them to ensure the longevity of your business. At first, this may seem straightforward, but it will take you out of your comfort zone and force you to make some tough decisions.

The Digital Jeweller Scorecard

What you can measure, you can improve upon.

I've created a great tool to help you analyse your current strengths and weaknesses against the Digital Jeweller method.

Before you continue reading, take the Digital Jeweller scorecard by visiting the link below.

www.thedigitaljeweller.com/scorecard

This set of questions is designed to score you against the four steps of the Digital Jeweller Method as described in this book. You will receive a customised report based on your answers.

The results of this scorecard will give you a starting point from which you can focus on the weaker areas of your business that need attention.

1. PREPARE

"By failing to prepare, you are preparing to fail."
Benjamin Franklin

To begin, we must analyse the current state of your business and plot out the path ahead to ensure its longevity and growth for years to come. By now, you will have taken the Digital Jeweller scorecard, which would have plotted you against the 4 Ps. If you have not yet completed the scorecard, be sure to do this before you continue reading. It is important to form an understanding of where your business is currently at, and to identify where it can be improved.

Given the industry is not what it once was, I expect your business is suffering in certain areas as a result. Preparation is the cornerstone to achieving success, and it will give you clearer directions for the path ahead.

Know Your Customer

You may find this section a little back to basics, but I often find that traditional jewellers have lost their way. They no longer know who they are actually trying to target their brand towards. They try to become all things to all people, which results in the customer being just as confused as they are.

You cannot be a pawn broker and a fine jewellery retailer, for example. The two types of stores are at completely opposite ends of the spectrum. A pawn broker specialises in pre-owned estate jewellery, and lending money on valuables. Their customers are looking to purchase a bargain, sell gold or borrow money. Fine jewellers, on the other hand, are most often frequented by consumers looking to purchase new items of jewellery as gifts or for special occasions, such as engagements and weddings.

Both types of businesses attract different kinds of customers, and these customers have different values, appetites and behavioural patterns. By analysing the common traits and behaviours of your ideal customers, you can further understand who they are and what motivates them to buy. Using this information, you have a better understanding of who they are, which will then directly impact every aspect of your business – from the pricing of your products, to the way you communicate in your marketing material.

Your customer profile is made up of three main categories: demographics, psychographics and geographics. For each category, listed below are some examples of questions that will help you identify your ideal client, and help you focus your energy and message on acquiring them.

Demographics
Their personal identity and circumstances

- Age
- Gender
- Race/Ethnicity
- Education Level
- Occupation
- Income
- Homeowner
- Marital and family status

Psychographics
Their behaviour and beliefs, including personality, hobbies, style and humour:

- Hobbies
- Interests
- Favourite TV shows, music, websites or media
- Likes/dislikes
- Spending habits
- Social media habits
- Ethical views

Geographics
Their location in relation to your store(s)
- Where do they live?
- What country?
- What county/state?
- What town?
- What catchment?

If you are a small business, I recommend profiling your ideal client in relation to the top three selling product categories in your business. You should then focus your initial efforts towards the segments of people you identify. As your business grows, you can revisit and segment more groups of customers with more focused products and services.

Be sure to access as much historical data as you can, as this will help you identify and understand the three key traits of your ideal customer. You should even talk directly to your best customers and ask them more about themselves and what they enjoy. The more similarities you can identify, the easier it will be to profile them.

Where Is Their Attention?

By understanding where your ideal customers spend most of their time, both physically and online, it can help form targeted advertising and marketing strategies, which will drive traffic and an awareness of your business.

- What other stores do they visit?
- What magazines do they read?
- What types of websites do they visit?
- What social media platforms do they use?
- What events do they attend?

One of the most successful marketing campaigns I have had, was as a direct result of profiling our ideal customers' attention. We identified that many of the brides who purchased from our stores had visited two well-known regional wedding fairs in our area. So we decided to take a small stand at each fair.

We then created a geofenced, targeted Facebook campaign that ensured all Facebook users who were engaged to be married and, who were within a mile radius of those fairs, would see our advert in their newsfeed.

Simply by identifying the behaviour and preferences of our ideal customer, we were able to create mass awareness through directly targeting the perfect consumers of our bridal products.

Know Your Customer Exercise

The best way to visualise your ideal customer is to create "his and her" personas, and even give them names and faces. A good way to do this is to do a quick Google search for "male and female model", then pick the two respective models faces you feel best represent your ideal clients. For this example, we'll call them Joe and Jane.

On a notepad, make a list of your best product categories and services.

- Pick the top three products and services from that list
- Choose your top service and start a separate page for both Joe and Jane
- List clear demographics for both
- List clear psychographics for both
- List clear geographics for both
- Then create separate lists of places that have their attention
- Repeat this for your two other chosen products or services

Notes

Empower Your Staff

Having a highly motivated team that understands the vision of the business is paramount to its success. Surround yourself with happy and energetic people, and you will find that passion and energy will find its way to your customers, too.

You should empower your staff with the tools and information they need to run the business without you. With this in place, you can step back and concentrate on working on the business, not in the business.

Document Your Processes

Your business processes should be documented so that, no matter what the situation, during the day to day operation, all members of staff are able to solve any process without having to seek advice from management.

The best place to start is to document every single process that is carried out on a daily, weekly and monthly basis. Encourage your team to take an analytical approach to their daily tasks, and create step by step instructions on how to perform a particular task. Tasks could range from how and where to order stationery for the office, to how to process refunds and payments using card terminals. Here are just a few tasks my team have documented in the past, some of which had videos recorded to bring further clarity to the task.

- How to create new product labels
- How to use the point of sale software

- How to engrave a ring using the designated machine
- How to process a refund on a gift card
- How to add additional stock to the stock database
- How to accurately measure a customer's finger

I recommend using the online cloud service called "Google Docs". It provides free business tools that help you create documents and spreadsheets, which are easily accessible from most web browsers on any internet-enabled device. Save the documents into clearly organised folders and give them easy to search file names. This will ensure quick and easy retrieval when a staff member needs to reference them. Google also gives joint access to a shared calendar so that multiple users can access it. It can be used as a central store calendar to schedule appointments, staff meetings and any events.

The aim of documenting the business processes is to help the company prepare for growth. It can also be used to train any new staff that have come into the business.

Internal Knowledge Base

The internal knowledge base is a valuable source of information for staff to access when facing uncertainty. A knowledge base is a repository of information slowly built over time as new information is added. Staff can access the knowledge base to resolve common issues found during the day to day running of a store. Each store should have its own knowledge base, as well as access to a central knowledge base for the wider company if there are multiple outlets.

Articles in the knowledge base should contain more product and service oriented information, which requires specific knowledge of the decisions already taken by management. Some example articles that my team have created can be found below:

- What are the contact details for the (insert brand here) account manager?
- What are the phone numbers for the other stores?
- What is the returns policy for earrings?
- Where is the preferred workshop for chain repairs?
- What to do when faced with an angry customer
- What discounts can be offered on certain product categories.

This should be a useful source of information that is constantly reviewed, edited and updated to ensure the latest and most accurate information is always saved. When staff ask questions regarding policies on how to make decisions on important subjects, capture them and add them to the knowledge base. You'll soon find that staff are happier as they can then solve any problems that arise themselves.

Knowledge base software is often part of a dedicated software solution for customer relationship management, but, usually, it's only for your customers to access. Ideally, you should use software that also includes an internal knowledge base for internal staff access only. If your chosen solution doesn't offer an internal knowledge base, then Google Docs is an alternative. It's a free solution where you can save articles in the cloud for all to access.

Visit docs.google.com for more information.

Staff Training

Staff training is often one of the most neglected areas of any business, but it is one of the most important. Having a solid training program for new starters will ensure that your products and services are sold with confidence. It will also reduce the number of questions and complaints received.

Training documents should include a base level of knowledge from which new recruits can grow their skills in the role they have come into. It's important to include basic information related to jewellery, as not all recruits will have prior knowledge of the jewellery industry.

Visual training aids are, by far, the best resource for new team members as they provide a much better understanding of how to implement what they're learning. This should be in the form of keynote presentations on specific topics, partnered with takeaway booklets containing the same information for their reference.

Here are a few recommended topics that work as a good starting framework for your training programme:

- Introduction to the company, its history and founders
- Customer profiles, etiquette and behaviour
- Standards and merchandising
- The jewellery production process
- Diamonds and gemstones
- Brands and watches
- Repairs and custom design

I recommend splitting the training into modules that run on a weekly basis to ensure the new recruit is not overloaded with information. Training on the job is the best way to bring a new staff member up to the required level. Be sure to celebrate milestones like their first day, their first sale and their first custom design.

The training program will need to be reviewed over time. You can update it when you feel that a training area is missing. We found that having a training manual ensured our existing staff had a reference point from which to structure training sessions for new staff members.

Developing an effective staff training program can even lead to a happier, more satisfied team, which, in turn, increases staff retention and reduces complaints from customers.

Monthly Reviews

Monthly reviews are a great way to ensure staff are listened to, and made to feel valued. They also form a great platform to receive feedback and recommendations, directly from the shop floor, on how the business can improve. Monthly reviews should be documented and include targets for staff to work on, which can then be discussed in the next review.

Here are some recommended Key Performance Indicators (KPI) that can be discussed and reviewed on a monthly basis with your management team:

- Last month's sales and targets
- Quarterly sales and targets
- Number of complaints and returns

- Staff training and store improvements
- Any commissions or incentive targets

Your management team should also hold monthly reviews with their team, and with individual staff members. It is important for managers to take the lead in the process, allowing staff members to go away and think about the areas they need to improve to help them become better salespersons. Managers should structure a monthly review process, give feedback on the team environment and be open to receive feedback on themselves. If done effectively, you will to have a happier and more energetic team as a result.

Empower Your Staff Exercise

The size of your business will typically dictate the amount of documentation you have currently amassed. It's important to start formalising and documenting your business activities and processes. It's equally important to continually update those documents and there's no better way than to build on them over time.

Here are some tasks you can initiate to ensure you have the right documents in place to help automate and scale your business:

- Create a shared Google drive so all staff have access to documents
- Save all new and existing documents within this shared folder
- Create a list of repetitive processes and document them
- Identify important information/contact details and document them
- Collate employee policies into a folder, ready to create a handbook
- Work with managers to identify training modules that would benefit all
- Set up dates for monthly reviews and KPIs in your shared calendar

Notes

Review Your Stock

One of the main advantages that digital jewellers have over traditional jewellers is that high value stock is kept to a minimum, freeing up much needed cash flow back into the business. This enables the business to be more fluid and dynamic with its product offering, and allows for it to curate more unique and varying product ranges.

Through leveraging the power of a digital inventory, a store that once had only 500 products on offer, can now offer thousands of products in millions of variations.

A traditional jeweller holds valuable pieces in different styles and qualities in stock, with a high percentage of costly bridal jewellery forming much of it. In today's economy, this is a strategy that is destined for failure. The businesses ability to perform will be severely limited unless it is backed by a very large bank balance or products given on consignment.

High value rings are impossible to stock in multiple finger sizes, resulting in the piece usually being stocked in a single finger size. Subsequently, when making a purchase, the customer is unable to take away the product the same day. Instead, they return a week or so later to collect the resized ring. If it has to be specially ordered from the supplier, it could even take up to 4-8 weeks for the item to be ready for collection.

A Digital Jeweller will only have to stock the necessary range of diamonds and gemstones to allow the consumer to make an informed decision on quality, before selecting their own stones on a screen from a digital inventory.

A choice can be made to stock designs in either silver with cubic zirconia (CZ), or alternatively with real diamond examples, with CZs to simulate the larger expensive stones. Either way, the reduction in stock value will improve the jeweller's ability to update their product offering faster, and with less reliance on having to turnover stock.

In the case of the high value rings mentioned above, it takes just 7-12 working days for a piece to be custom made exactly to the customer's specification, without the piece having to be cut and resized. The ring is made as a solid piece, increasing the longevity of the item, resulting in a higher quality product than one that is resized.

Whilst I'm not saying that you should strip your business of all its most valuable products, I am advising that it would be beneficial to review your current stock holding. Determine what you can remove so that you can utilise the cash in more productive ways within your business, rather than it just sitting in your shop window.

Reducing Stock = Faster Returns

My top performing retail store was opened in the one of the UK's largest shopping destinations, Bluewater Kent, in the South East of England. It had a floor space of only 192 sq. ft., just 16 x 12 ft. in size.

The store was stocked with over 400 silver and CZ sample rings to allow customers to touch and feel the products, in addition to a small selection of real diamonds and gemstone rings of different sizes and qualities. It cost just £30,000 to fit out the store with custom made cabinets, including the cost of all the required stock.

From the first month of trading, we took in revenues in excess of £100,000 every month, which equates to revenue in excess of £6,000 per sq. ft. per year, a figure surpassing Tiffany & Co, and very close to Apple. Within three months, the store had recouped its opening costs and started to return a profit to the company.

The reason the store was so successful was due to its low operational costs, which increased the return on the investment (ROI). We resisted the temptation to fill the store with £250,000 worth of stock and, in return, we were rewarded with a break-even point just three months from opening.

By leveraging a digital inventory, 95% of sales are made to order, meaning we are not holding any unwanted stock. Yet, customers still have the choice of thousands of product variations.

Due to the size of the store, we decided that this store would specialise in bridal and high value jewellery. Although, it is important to point out that gift products should not be ignored. A good selection of gifts products should be stocked by jewellers with a retail store as there will be demand from the local community, who rely on your store for convenient gift purchases.

This particular store was open for five years but, due to the increasing rent and steady decline in footfall at the shopping centre, it was clear that a renewal of the lease would not be a sound business decision. I believe large shopping malls are no longer suitable locations for retail jewellers due to the increasing rents and falling footfalls.

Gift Purchases

For any jeweller with a retail store, stocking products that can be purchased and taken away immediately, should form part of your core offering. For bricks and mortar stores with high footfall, gift purchases are an absolute must to maintain that footfall. This strategy will also reinforce great relationships with customers. You need to be known in your locality as the place to go and buy great jewellery gifts. Stock a variety of brands and more unique pieces at low price points. Make it really easy for customers to pick up their gifts and run out the door with them. These are the opportunity sales that will keep money flowing through the till, and keep the staff busy. Don't lose them.

The digital inventory model should consist of products that can be easily customised and personalised, where the customer is happy to wait a short lead time for their purchase. Generally, this applies to most bridal, diamond jewellery and rings, where the purchase price is high. Customers are usually happy to wait for the piece to be made specially for them.

Review Your Stock Exercise

It's time to review your stock holding and free up much needed cash, which can be saved for a rainy day or put towards growth.

- Start by doing a stock take of your current inventory to get an accurate understanding of your stock holding today
- Identify and list the items of stock you have had for more than a year
- Identify and list all items which are always made to order, even though you have stock
- Identify and list all stock that contains diamonds over 0.25ct, which could easily be replaced with a CZ to help reduce the value of your stock
- Consider scrapping any stock that has not sold in over two years, and use the components for orders you receive over time

Notes

Reduce Your Overheads

Rent and Taxes

With rent and property taxes continuing to rise in the commercial landscape, it is important to review your current situation in relation to your business locations, and do so on a yearly basis.

As a jewellery retailer, I have had my fair share of ups and downs with store locations. If there is one piece of advice I can give you in this current climate, it is not to commit your business to a lease of more than five years. Also, insist on a break clause at least halfway through the term. This will give you the flexibility to adapt and change your business model as time goes on, allowing you the freedom to close locations if the economic climate becomes unfavourable for whatever reason.

It's clear that the consumer is spending more time online than in a store environment, which is why shopping malls are struggling to keep retailers.[4] Lower footfall and high running costs make shopping mall units even harder to justify. Having to pay staff to cover the extended opening hours that malls demand is another reason that mall units are harder to sustain.

The traditional high street is a place that has also been on the decline over many years. High vacancy rates have continued, and the number of high quality stores that

---

4 https://www.statista.com/topics/2333/e-commerce-in-the-united-kingdom/

remain have fallen.[5] Smaller towns and villages are, on the other hand, thriving with independent stores, which are building strong roots within the community. Think about your position in the local community, and how you can leverage lower rental prices in smaller towns so you can grow your following and have customers come to you if they wish to buy in person rather than online.

Don't be scared to make bold decisions when it comes to your retail locations. If you are seeing a steady decline in sales, but an increase in online sales and appointments, think about ways you can lower your overheads. Could you change the location of your store to a unit that has lower rent? Could you switch from a retail store to a showroom? Should you renew the lease on a store that is not as profitable as it once was?

Many factors will play a role in the future profitability of your store, with rent being one of the biggest and more considerable overheads in your business.

Staff

By far, though, the largest overhead in your business is your staff. Staff numbers should be carefully planned to ensure the company is getting the most from its employees whilst also making a profit.

A metric often used to analyse the productivity of your business is its revenue per full-time employee. Businesses with a high revenue per employee enjoy better cash

---

5 https://www.telegraph.co.uk/business/2017/01/08/online-retail-booms-high-street-struggles/

flows, higher profit margins and growth. Those with a low revenue per employee experience tougher trading conditions and struggle to grow.

To calculate your current revenue per employee, count the number of full-time staff, then add together the total number of hours worked by part-time staff in a single week. If the sum of part-time staff hours exceeds 40 hours per week, this is counted as another full-time employee. To calculate your revenue per employee, divide last year's turnover figure by the number of employees, including yourself.

Revenue per employee = net revenue/number of full-time employees

As a benchmark, digital jewellers should be aiming for an annual revenue per employee that is greater than £150,000. Anything below this and the company will struggle to make a profit once company directors are paid their salaries.

If you want to understand more about revenue per employee, read *24 Assets* by Daniel Priestley – http://www.dent.global/thedigitaljeweller

It's now common to see traditional retail jewellers with revenues below £100,000 per employee, and this is a stressful place to be. Overheads will be eating into any profit made, leaving little left to pay the owner. If you find yourself in this position, it's time to think seriously about changing your business model to ensure the longevity of your business, and your own health!

Insurance

The jewellery industry is commonly targeted by thieves looking for high value items, so insurance premiums are a necessary expense for jewellers. Insurance is another large overhead a traditional jeweller faces due to the volume of high value stock held.

By taking advantage of a digital inventory, you can drastically reduce the amount of stock held, which will, in turn, considerably reduce the premium sought by your insurer. It is truly amazing how low the insurance premium is in comparison to stores stocked with lots of high value items.

I recommend you contact the account manager at your insurance broker to discuss the different ways you can reduce the cost of your insurance premium. Even simple things like increasing your insurance excess and reducing your public liability cover could help reduce the cost.

Also, consider shopping around for new insurance quotations. It's easy to get comfortable with your insurer, especially when you rarely speak to them.

Advertising

Advertising is an area that can quickly eat away at your bottom line, unless it is carefully managed. By advertising smartly, you will be able to reduce the cost of your advertising whilst increasing the reach of your message.

Print Advertising

The traditional jeweller has long favoured advertising in the local newspaper. But, when you can't measure the effectiveness of your campaigns, it's very difficult to know if what you're spending is good value for money. Philadelphia retailer John Wanamaker supposedly said: "Half the money I spend on advertising is wasted; the trouble is, I don't know which half." This quote is still relevant to all print advertising done today, where results cannot be accurately measured.

That doesn't mean you shouldn't spend any money on print advertising. If you own a bricks and mortar store and have a good local presence, it's certainly something you should continue with, but on a smaller scale. That way, your brand and name is still triggered in people's minds as they flick through the local newspaper.

If you don't have a high street location, then I don't recommend you spend any of your advertising budget on print advertising. Instead, stay with digital advertising, with the aim of driving traffic to your website and your showroom.

Digital Advertising

Before you run any digital advertising campaigns, ensure you speak to a professional. Pay-per-click (PPC) advertising campaigns should be overseen by professionals to ensure you are getting the most from your advertising spend, and not wasting money.

It's very easy to overspend on digital marketing as people are very click happy these days. If you don't place a limit on your spend, and you don't drill down to a very targeted niche range of keywords, your marketing budget will easily exceed your actual income. I've seen people waste thousands of pounds on digital marketing because they've been sold a package that promises great results. Seek advice from a professional company. Set limits on your spending and keep an eye on your conversion rates. In a later chapter dedicated to digital marketing, I'll show you how to make the most of your digital campaigns.

Other Expenses

The remainder of your overheads are likely to be smaller, routine purchases like stationary, packaging and office equipment.

The business world is becoming more competitive and consumers are spending their money further and wider afield than ever before. So, it's important to analyse your smaller expenses, too. Do you really need to spend thousands of pounds on the latest Apple computer? Do you really need those Mont Blanc pens? Just because you like a brand, it doesn't mean it's the best purchase choice for your business. Remember, when purchasing anything for your business, a pen is a pen. Can you source a lower cost version of a product that will do the same job without sacrificing quality?

Where possible, buy second-hand office equipment. A second-hand purchase will always do the same job as a new one. When you're starting or growing a business, every penny counts towards improving your bottom line. So be sure to analyse all expenses, no matter how small.

Reduce Overheads Exercise

This is not the easiest exercise to undertake, but reducing the overheads in your business can only contribute to greater profits. That much is certain.

Here are a few ways to look at reducing your overheads:

- Calculate the monthly cost of your rent and rates/taxes of your business properties
- Calculate your monthly staff costs per location, including any government and pension scheme payments
- Now calculate the break-even figure for each location
- Review your insurance premium and ask for quotes for reduced coverage
- Get similar quotes from other insurance companies
- Review your monthly advertising spend for both print and digital
- Identify and list any unnecessary overheads that can be removed

Notes

Embrace Technology

Traditional jewellers often have a limited digital offering and online presence. Some don't even have a simple website. Consumers spend more time looking at their mobile phones than at any other screen. As such, you need to embrace software and systems that allow you to reach a wider audience, and serve them better.

A Digital Jeweller embraces the latest technology available to automate as much of their business as possible. By doing so, they can serve a greater number of customers and increase the number of sales they can process. This, in turn, reduces the cost per acquisition.

You may not be able to find a software provider that provides an all-in-one solution, but here are the main types of software that I recommend you apply to your business as soon as possible:

Customer Relationship Management – CRM

Also known as a CRM solution, customer relationship management is the industry standard cloud based software used to manage interactions with your customers. Communications with your customers should be visible to all staff members, including information about your customers, a detailed history of all previous communications, orders and number of visits to your website.

By recording information about every interaction the customer has with your business, including order dates, the reason for a purchase and who made the purchase, you start to build up a comprehensive record. This will help staff provide a more personal service and allow them to retrieve information about customers on demand.

Imagine having the ability to automatically remind your customer of their upcoming anniversary next month, making product recommendations in advance of the event. Keeping an in-depth record of this kind of relevant information on your customers, built up over time, will give you a competitive advantage in a future where businesses are competing for loyalty and referrals.

Multi-Channel Communication

There are many ways consumers can contact your business. Given this, it is important to consider simple ways to communicate with your customers through multiple channels. Technology now allows you to speak to them via a single interface, no matter the platform or communication channel. Email, SMS, WebChat, Facebook, Twitter, Instagram and LinkedIn are just a few platforms through which customers send their enquiries.

Facebook is by far the most popular and preferred platform for consumers to interact with businesses, as it's also where most of their social communication takes place. The Facebook messenger app processes over 2 billion messages every month and is used by over 11% of the world's population.[6] This free tool is therefore one of the main ways

---

6 https://www.statista.com/statistics/417295/facebook-messenger-monthly-active-users/

consumers interact with your business. This trend is likely to grow as more people join the Facebook platform.

Your chosen CRM software should include the ability to communicate through multiple channels as standard, with email and Facebook being channels that are required without question. Be sure to take the time to evaluate the different features of a CRM before signing up to one as it can be difficult to change software once you have made a commitment.

Website Management System

Your website is the most important element of your business as a digital jeweller. It's important to choose the right provider and technology, ensuring your website and digital product listings are simple and easy to manage. This is a very important decision and should be taken with care.

Ideally, your website should integrate seamlessly with your customer relationship management system and your multi-channel communication system. By doing so, you are able see much more information via a single interface, therefore giving your customers a more seamless experience as a result.

Effectively, your website management system should be running your business and generating ongoing revenue and enquiries, so be sure to take your time when evaluating the right platform.

Voice Over IP Telephony

Growing in popularity, VOIP is an internet based telephone system that allows advanced call routing, call queuing and multi-contact phone numbers. This plug and play solution works entirely over the internet and is quick and easy to set-up.

When a customer calls your phone number, hoping to speak to someone in your business, it can be quite frustrating to hear a busy tone instead. It's quite likely you'll end up with an upset client and a lost sale. By adding a queuing system to your business, your staff can handle multiple calls simultaneously, and they will never miss a call again.

There are many VOIP providers, so my suggestion would be to make a choice based on the cost of set-up, the call packages on offer and the user-friendliness of the interface. Some VOIP interfaces can be very confusing and difficult for staff to learn and navigate, so be sure to ask for a demonstration before signing a contract.

Cloud Accounting

One of the most recent advances in accounting technology was the release of cloud accounting. Cloud accounting is one of the best technologies we applied to our business, and it has helped streamline a lot of our accounting tasks. Bank feeds allow direct connection between your business bank account and your accounting software, eliminating the need for manual entry and allowing for automatic reconciliation. This single feature alone has saved us from the task of inputting data from statements and reconciling them with our bank account; once a very time-consuming job.

Quickbooks (Intuit.com) and Xero (Xero.com) are clear market leaders in this space. I have used both for my businesses. Each have their pros and cons, but both allow your accountant to login remotely to access your data and perform any tasks required.

I'd recommend discussing this with your accountant, then initiate the process of making the change as soon as you can.

Insights

It's very important to make informed business decisions based on the data your business generates. All technology providers should provide deep insights based on your sales data, the effectiveness of your marketing and the conversion rate of your digital marketing strategy.

Google Analytics is an industry standard tool for obtaining deeper insights on the performance of your website, and information about visitors. By adding analytics code to your website, you can start tracking every visitor and collect huge amounts of useful data, such as the devices they are using and pages they are visiting on your website.

Here are a few performance indicators you should be reporting on every month via your chosen software solution. This will help you make more informed decisions on your business strategy.

- Sales
- Profit and loss
- Product margins
- Website visitors
- Conversion rates
- Average cart value
- Cost per acquisition

The most valuable insights come from the reports on your sales data within your software. By segmenting your product categories and analysing the sales over time, you can monitor which categories are increasing, what products sales are increasing and those that are in decline. Use these valuable insights to inform your decisions on the future strategy of your business and your product selection.

An omnichannel sales system should be used to ensure point of sale and online sales are captured in a single software interface, making it easier to identify which products are stronger than others, both online and in store. This will provide deeper insights on the best brands and products to invest in going forward.

Basically, the more data you put in, the better your business insights. Through the use of advanced point of sale and online software, and capturing that data, you can draw meaningful insights.

A Common Mistake!

I've come across hundreds of traditional jewellers who have fallen into the trap set by generic technology providers. Traditional jewellers believe that, with these tools, they'll receive a quality final product. However, traditional jewellers are not at fault here. Some technology providers are convinced they can apply technology that was designed for a different industry to the jewellery industry.

Another common error is choosing a website provider and platform that was not designed for the jewellery industry. This, however, applies to most website platforms available today.

I've seen jewellers spend thousands of pounds on the promise of a brilliant website, one that will change their fortunes. The reality they soon come to realise, is that operating a website and changing the prices of hundreds of products daily is near impossible with a standard website management system.

The root of the problem is that most standard website platforms cater for fixed price products that have few variables. For example, a T-Shirt available in five sizes. Most retail industries that sell directly to consumers offer fixed price products in a similar way.

For fashion led products, this software is fine as the prices are fixed. The software is designed specifically for these kinds of products: high volume and low price. The jewellery industry, on the other hand, deals with products of higher value. Most of which are made to order, with far more variables. This kind of software does not meet the jewellers' business requirements, and fails to provide a remarkable solution.

The jewellery industry deals with products where the price changes frequently due to fluctuations in precious metals and diamond prices. To cater for this frequent fluctuation, price adjustments needs to be automated; a function standard website platforms do not offer.

Traditional jewellers are therefore forced down the route of listing fixed price products online. Potentially, there will be a negative impact on the profit within a sale when the value of precious metals and diamonds increase. There is also a chance of lost sales as consumers can only see the product available in a single metal and single stone size, sometimes without even the option to choose a finger size!

A Digital Jeweller embraces industry specific software that is designed to resolve this issue. With a single click of a button, they can publish a digital product on their website. The product can be priced and visualised with thousands of different variables, whilst being linked directly to the supplier for instant pricing updates.

This direct connection also means that when an order is placed, the supplier also receives the order automatically. Subsequently, the product is created and delivered to the store as per the customer's specification, without the need for any manual processing.

Embrace Technology Exercise

It's time to research the different software solutions available to help you streamline and automate your retail business.

Here are a few exercises that will help you identify the different solutions:

- Make a shortlist of software solutions for the following categories:
  Customer Relationship Management, Multi-Channel Communication, Website Hosting and Management, VOIP Telephony, Cloud Accounting

- List the pros and cons for each software
- Share your list and review with colleagues
- Schedule a demo with your chosen providers
- Ask for links to relevant training portals
- Focus on a single software at a time so as not to overwhelm your staff

Notes

Preparations Have Begun

I've now covered the key business areas that you will need to review and change, in preparation for the ongoing digital disruption. The digital jeweller scorecard would have also indicated the weaker areas of your business for you to work on.

It may seem like a daunting task initially, but as you plan the steps to execute over time, you will realise that, with some persistence your goals can be achieved.

Let technology do the leg work for you, and ensure your team fully understands the new technology being implemented within your business. Schedule internal training sessions with your staff, and update your documentation accordingly.

Now that preparations are underway, it's time to understand the theory of automated production, and apply modern manufacturing methods that will supercharge your business and the value it offers.

2. PRODUCE

"When the tools of production are available to everyone, everyone becomes a producer."
Chris Anderson, author of *The Long Tail: Why the future is selling less of more*

Prior to the internet, the world was a very different place. Consumers had a limited number of products on offer in retail stores, most of which specialised in specific product categories. Larger stores, known as department stores, consisted of lots of different departments offering all types of products. These department stores still exist today.

Retail stores were the only option available to the consumer, and business was good. In both cases, the products on offer were curated by buyers, who selected the most suitable products for their stores. Some products turned out to be hits and sold in huge quantities. Many other products, however, catered to a more niche category and had fewer sales. These products were eventually discontinued and replaced by new products hoping to be hits.

Today, the internet allows consumers to search across vast volumes of products, which, effectively, are rarely discontinued. Millions of small niches exist, selling smaller quantities of unique products, and consumers are searching farther and wider year on year.

The jewellery industry is no different. Consumers are now discovering designers, brands and fine jewellers they never knew existed. It's simply no longer viable to curate a small collection of products offered by wholesalers. Fine jewellery is just too expensive to stock in an increasing variety of unique designs in the hopes they will sell.

Digital jewellers must leverage technology to curate a digital inventory of fine jewellery made by designers from around the world. Digital products cost very little to stock online. They can also be manufactured to the unique specification of the customer.

Curate a Digital Inventory

A digital inventory is a list of non-physical digital products that can be sold to a consumer by manufacturing them on request. These products are often stored in 3D format and 3D printed to realise their form in the physical world, before post processing.

It is difficult to envisage how a digital inventory will fully replace a mainstream mass produced product. And, it is true that some products are simply too popular to sell without the physical stock to cater for demand. However, there is a genuine case for a digital inventory, not only from a business standpoint, but from an environmental and sustainable one.

By intelligently managing your physical stock, whilst supported by a digital inventory, you can considerably reduce the stock holding in your company. In turn, this will drastically reduce the amount of waste production and inventory write off. This can have a huge impact on your bottom line, providing the much needed cash for other resources in this increasingly competitive market.

The jewellery industry is one of the first major industries that is ripe for disruption from the use of digital inventories. Presently, nearly all fine jewellery is made from a 3D model. With the reduction in the cost of 3D printing, it is now just as cost effective to 3D print a wax model for direct casting, as it is to create a rubber mould for mass production.

This means that the cost of making one piece is similar to the cost of making 10, 50 or 100 pieces of the same product. The post-processing is the same, and it takes the same length of time to finish each piece.

In the case of purchasing a ring, it is rare for you to stock the combination of finger size and ring design the consumer wishes to buy. It's too costly to stock the same ring in 25 different sizes to try and cater for every eventuality. So, the correct size needs to be sourced from a different store (if you have others). This can take a week or so to organise. More commonly, though, it is ordered from a traditional supplier, and this can take anywhere from 4-8 weeks.

Enter the digital inventory model, where a retailer is able to sell a product in thousands of different variations. This model allows for customisation of a product by offering a selection of different metals and gemstones, that can be visualised on screen with the consumer. The customised ring design is then delivered to the store in a matter of days, custom made to the correct finger size and specification.

One single product SKU is now available in thousands of different combinations, and delivered within a short space of time to the consumer. Not only does a digital inventory drastically increase the volume of SKUs on offer, but it also increases customer satisfaction as it allows mass customisation and personalisation of every product.

What This Means for the Digital Jeweller

A digital jeweller uses a mix of physical and digital inventories. They showcase the more popular products in store, while customising and personalising anything on screen. The internet has opened up access to an almost infinite number of producers and, subsequently, there is infinite choice. A digital inventory will support the retailer's physical inventory, catering for an almost infinite choice of designs and customisable options, also known as the long tail.

Digital designers can create jewellery designs at almost zero cost, apart from the cost of the 3D modelling software and their time. Being a digital file, retailers can show products created by jewellery designers from around the world, without taking the risk of purchasing stock that may not sell. Only when an order is received is the product manufactured to a high standard by the manufacturer of choice.

Traditional jewellers often visit trade exhibitions to buy high value stock to display in store. Digital jewellers, however, look for new designs to display on their websites, and share on social media, by visiting online digital marketplaces. The considerable reduction in the cost of displaying an item in their stores allows the digital jeweller to test the market with a new product line through feedback from followers on social media.

It's Time To Move to a Digital Inventory Model

I expect you have many thoughts on how you could move your business towards a digital inventory model. You'll have stock of many designs, which are one-off pieces. It's also likely that you'll have expensive diamonds that have been sitting in your window for some time.

To effectively initiate this gradual shift towards a leaner approach, utilise the components of your stock as and when you get orders for them. For example, if you have an engagement ring in stock that has a 1.00ct G VS2 round brilliant diamond set into it, but you receive an order for a F VS2. Speak to the customer and offer them the chance to upgrade. You'll find this usually goes down very well with your customer, whilst reducing your stock holding.

When it comes to pricing existing stock in different metals, I recommend that you work with suppliers that give you the flexibility to price designs instantly for multiple metals and stone qualities where appropriate. A Digital Jeweller will not stock any product that cannot be priced in multiple variations, apart from low value stock intended as gift purchases the consumer, so that they can take away the product at the time of purchase.

Moving to a digital inventory model will not happen overnight. I recommend that you plan the transition to happen over a period of 12 months. This transition, however, will see your business become a leaner and more adaptable business, whilst also improving the cash balance of your bank account.

Curate a Digital Inventory - Exercise
To curate a digital inventory, first identify your core range of best selling products that could easily become digital products.

- Create a list of your core product categories, which you can transfer to a digital inventory and have made to order
- Identify new styles you could easily add to your product offering, styles that would fit in seamlessly with your core product categories
- Create a list of products you would like to offer, but haven't offered due to the cost of stocking them as real pieces
- Create a list of 12 product collections that you can curate over the next 12 months, releasing a new collection of products monthly

Notes

Customisation

Customisation is by far the most value adding benefit of embracing a digital inventory. It significantly increases consumer satisfaction and reduces returns. The core of your fine jewellery offering should consist of products made from digital files that can be customised and visualised on screen in thousands of possible combinations of metals, gemstones and diamonds. Bridal jewellery, in particular, should not be limited to the single metal and stone size it is stocked in.

If you offer a customised option alongside the traditional method of stocking a product, which is only available in one variable, the consumer will opt for the custom option 95% of the time. There is truly nothing as powerful as selling a product that has been made explicitly for the customer, to their specification. The purchase is no longer just a transaction, it becomes an experience. It is this experience they will share with the world on social media.

When you break a product down into its components, it's clear which parts can be customised simply by separating the pricing of that component. Today's technology allows for instant calculation of any combination of parts, with minimal effort. Just as you can customise the colour and interior of your car, a Digital Jeweller allows you to customise the components of your jewellery.

Here are a few popular customisations that are available to Digital Jewellers today:

Precious Metals

Offering a product in different metals should be the easiest type of customisation to offer. Many traditional jewellers, however, struggle to price products in multiple metals. Silver, platinum and gold of all colours can change the value of a piece considerably, offering a variety of price points for any budget, and a great way to upsell the customer.

Certified Diamonds

The internet has given rise to a few popular certified diamond markets that list thousands of diamonds from suppliers all over the world. This makes it easier to offer consumers the ability to customise their jewellery with their own choice of certified diamonds. Engagement rings, especially, are popular products where the main stone is often chosen by the consumer from the worldwide digital inventory of diamonds.

Gemstones

Coloured stones come in every shade known to man, offering more choice and options to customise colour than with any other part of a piece of jewellery. Traditionally, it has been difficult for jewellers to offer such an extensive customisation. Instead, they resort to requesting a selection of gemstones from a gemstone dealer, hoping their description of the colour desired by the consumer is understood.

Digital jewellers allow for the consumer to search an almost infinite database of coloured gemstones from suppliers around the world. Precious and semi-precious gemstones can be visualised in high definition, allowing a detailed inspection on screen, as if it were in their hand.

Instant Matching

By the year 2020, I expect we'll see a huge central marketplace of digital inventory. The data from these products will interact and further increase the efficiency of the manufacturing pipeline, as well as increase the choice available to consumers.

Rather than having to source a certain gemstone to fit a certain design, technology will facilitate the perfect match of gem measurements to digital designs, and vice versa. Utilising the measurement data of both the real stone size and the 3D virtual stone in the 3D file, algorithms can recommend the best suited stones based on the user's selections and criteria.

By viewing a digital design in a certain variable, a list of perfectly fitting stones will show in the existing 3D model; a perfect example of digital assortment. The user then simply selects their preferred stone to be set into the ring. Behind the scenes, the manufacturing and fulfilment happens automatically.

Customisation Exercise

Let's identify the types of customisation wish to offer your customers.

- What precious metals would you offer?
- What diamond qualities would you offer?
- What gemstones would you offer?
- From where would you offer a selection of certified diamonds?
- Would you offer the customer to view a selection of stones in person?

Notes

Personalisation

Personalisation gives the consumer the option to add sentimental value to an item of jewellery they are purchasing for themselves or for a loved one.

Engraving is, by far, the most popular form of personalisation. By adding names or messages to an item of jewellery, the wearer forms an emotional bond to it. The perceived value, therefore, increases, allowing jewellers to charge a higher price for the product.

As with any product that has added emotional value, personalised products allow for higher margins. As a Digital Jeweller, personalisation should be an additional offering for as many products as possible. Ideally, without having to add to the lead time of production.

Personalised offerings could be as simple as a printed card within the gift box presented to the customer. Creating a simple interface during the ordering process to capture their personalised message is a great way to add value to your customers' experience.

Types of Jewellery Personalisation

Technology is slowly allowing for new forms of personalisation to be applied to jewellery in ways not seen before. Below, I have covered the main types of personalisation available today. As technology advances, I expect we'll see more unique and innovative ways to personalise jewellery.

Hand Engraving

Engraving has long been a traditional form of personalisation for all types of jewellery. Although, it is not as popular as it once was. Originally, hand engraving was the only personalisation option available. This was, and still is, an expensive way to engrave a piece of jewellery as it is labour intensive, requiring a skilled engraver to work on a piece by hand. However, there are fewer hand engravers in the industry due to the rise in machine personalisation. Hand engraving is now seen as a more romantic and higher quality form of engraving, primarily due to the more artisan feel of the finished piece. It is still worth considering hand engraving as an offering if you have access to a local skilled engraver, but ensure your customer knows of the extended lead time required to personalise a piece in this way.

Machine Engraving

Machine engraving was the next iteration of engraving and it has gained popularity. The beauty of machine engraving is that, with little or no maintenance, you can get a great machine to last many years, one that delivers consistently, year after year. The other benefit of machine engraving is that it is easy to remove errors made by a staff member. A quick sandpapering of the engraved area smooths down the engraving and allows for it to be re-engraved.

I, myself, have had the same machine engraver in our store for the last decade. It still does a great job, although the computer software is just as old! The machine I speak of is the RM4, which has now been superseded by the

IRM4. Visit Gravograph.com for more information on this reliable machine.

Laser Engraving

The latest form of engraving machinery is a laser marking machine, which applies a crisp and easy to read mark on any piece of jewellery. Laser marking has the benefit of allowing very small and minute marks to be made on products, unlike traditional and machine engraving.

The downside of laser engraving is that the machinery currently costs in the region of £15-25k, so it can be an expensive asset to have. Ideally, your supplier should offer laser engraving with the products it offers. So, with an additional minimal charge, you could also offer this form of personalisation.

The Assay Office in Birmingham is one such supplier that offers laser engraving with the submission of articles for hallmarking. This can be a streamlined way to get your items hallmarked and laser engraved at the same time, if you are having to submit your items for assay in the UK.

Handwriting

Along with the introduction of laser marking has come the ability to personalise jewellery with the customers' handwriting. There is nothing more personal than a handwritten message added to a piece of jewellery from a loved one.

The process works by asking the customer to write their message on a piece of white paper in a black ink, then take a picture of it with a mobile phone. This image is then uploaded to an online interface, which converts the black and white line drawing into a digital version. This is then overlaid onto the item of jewellery for the customer to visualise and approve. The handwriting can then be laser marked onto the jewellery piece in any orientation, as per the customer's specification.

It's important to note that the handwriting needs to fit within the boundaries of the piece. For example, for a ring, the handwriting should be written within a scaled-up version of the inside band. When scaled back down, it should still be legible.

Fingerprint

A fingerprint applied to jewellery is another trend that has been growing over recent years due to laser marking advances. We see this more often with wedding rings, as a gesture of commitment to one another applied to the inside or outside of the ring.

The process works by asking the customer to push their desired finger into a black ink pad, and then roll their finger onto a white piece of paper. The resulting black and white fingerprint is then captured with a mobile phone camera and uploaded to an online interface. Like the handwriting method above, this black and white image is then converted into a digital version, which is then overlaid onto the item of jewellery for the customer to visualise and approve before the piece is laser marked.

Heartbeat

One of the latest forms of personalisation currently on offer is the ability to capture a person's heartbeat, and apply it to a piece of jewellery.

Using a high definition smartphone camera, or a dedicated heartbeat device, the pulse from a user's finger can be inspected and measured, producing a pulse wave. The pulse wave can then be exported as a black and white line drawing and marked onto a piece.

This very personal act of placing your own heartbeat onto a gift for loved ones reaches a level of personalisation never seen before.

There is a growing demand for personalised jewellery and, as a digital jeweller, you should be using technology to make it easier for your customers to personalise their purchases.

Personalisation Exercise

At a minimum, you should be offering some form of engraving to allow customers to personalise many of the products you sell.

- Make a list of the types of personalisation you would like to offer your customers
- Identify which suppliers can personalise the products you purchase from them
- Request prices and examples of the personalisation available
- If you have a store, consider purchasing a machine engraver to offer a quick personalisation service in store
- Test different price points to see where the pushback point is for your personalisation charges, and maximise your returns

Notes

Custom Design

Traditionally, custom design was thought of as an expensive option to offer a customer. Before the availability of 3D design software, jewellery was mostly made by hand, a process that often took hours or even days to finish a piece.

The traditional method of carving wax by hand was a profession in itself. It took years to master. The main issue with this method was the length of time it took to create the wax models and, if a mistake was made during the carving process, the job would need to be restarted from scratch.

I vividly remember manufacturing jewellery fully by hand. All it took was an extra second of heat from the jeweller's torch to deform a piece, and I would have to start again. When training as a goldsmith, this was the most frustrating part of the job. Especially after putting hours of time and effort into a single piece, only to have it scrapped due to a slip of the wrist.

3D Modelling has become the standard tool for custom designed jewellery, and it has a very useful feature called the back button! As with wax carving, the software is difficult to master, and is also considered a profession in its own right. 3D Modellers often take years to become skilled modellers, creating the most complex geometric designs.

Many manufacturers still quote high prices for the creation of a custom design, often more than £100. This usually reflects their inefficient processes, lack of automation and high overheads. Subsequently, traditional jewellers often shy away from custom design due the perceived expense of starting the process for the consumer, when, in fact, it costs very little.

A Digital Jeweller embraces custom design as an additional offering, alongside customisation. Today, it is just as easy and cost effective to commission a new digital design, as it is to adjust an existing one. Platforms exists that network freelance 3D Modellers with jewellers who want low-cost, high quality 3D models created.

For example, at Cadfolio.com, a platform that I founded, for a small fee of around £30, a freelance 3D Modeller will create a 3D model from your sketches or images, then share a link for you to customise and price it instantly online, along with stunning visualisations of the design. The platform analyses the 3D model and extracts all the information required to price the product, whilst also creating professional renders to show your customers.

With a single click, the design can be forwarded to your customer via email/SMS, including a link to your website for them to customise and price it with your margin applied. If happy, your customer can then order their design online and production will start immediately. No 3D files have to be handled, nor is there a need for manual pricing calculations. The whole process is fully automated.

Compare this to the traditional method of sending multiple emails back and forth with a traditional manufacturer, where you have no idea of pricing or how to share it with your customer. This is a great demonstration of how automation can drastically cut back on the cost and lead time of producing a new piece of jewellery from scratch.

Once a new model is created, it becomes a digital product just like any other. It can be customised, adjusted and personalised just like any existing product before it. Digital products are more fluid than traditional fixed price products, and can take on many variations and even inspire new products.

Jewellery design is becoming a continuous, evolving mix of styles and ideas that are constantly interwoven with each other. As a Digital Jeweller, you should not be afraid to let existing designs influence your own creations.

3D Modelling (CAD Design)

Trying to learn 3D Modelling yourself is like taking up a new professional skill set. It is a skill that takes years to master, and reach an advanced level. Yet, it still it takes hours to create a new design from scratch. I've seen many businesses buy expensive software licenses only to discover that, to become a competent 3D Modeller, it takes years of practice.

Unless you can dedicate at least 20 hours per week to learning how to create 3D models yourself using 3D Modelling software, I recommend you employ skilled freelancers to create the 3D models.

Using multiple freelancers will allow you to manage multiple custom design jobs at the same time, which then allows you to scale the number of orders you can process. Your only limitation is the number of freelancers available to do the work.

Using freelancers to create 3D models must also be a streamlined and automated process. Your aim as a Digital Jeweller is to reduce the amount of time you spend per order so you can process more orders in less time, and increase your bottom line profit as a result.

The Five Steps of Successful Custom Design

Before starting the custom design process with a customer, I recommend requesting payment from them to cover the CAD design charges, something in the region of £35-50. By requesting payment in advance, you still cover your costs in the event the customer decides not to proceed. It also filters out any time wasters.

I have tested multiple price points in retail stores, for what we call the "design fee". Anything above £50 and customers start to push back as they see it as an expensive upfront cost for a process they are not 100% sure about.

Never discount this cost off the final price. This is always charged as an upfront payment to cover the 3D CAD design charges. It is good to explain to the customer that, in return, they get stunning imagery of the design they wish to order. Try testing your customers with different price points to see what you could ideally charge before you get push back.

Once you have secured a design fee in advance from your customer, you can then start the five-step custom design process with them.

1. Discover

Discovery is the first stage of the custom design process. The objective of this stage is to determine what your client is hoping to achieve from the process, and what their desired end result may look like.

I often meet customers who have no idea of what they want to create. They just want something "nice and unique" for their wife or partner.

Starting with a question and answer session is the best way to determine the ideal objective of the custom design process. This also ensures that the end goal is achieved to the highest satisfaction.

I recommend using a combination of the questions below to help focus your client's request. Doing so will help them feel like they have had input in the creation of the custom designed piece or set.

- Who is the piece of jewellery for?
- What type of jewellery do you want designed? Ring, pendant, earrings, a set?
- What colour metal does your partner usually wear?
- Does your partner like bold, large pieces or small, delicate pieces?
- What is your partner's birthstone?
- What is your partner's favourite colour?
- Does your partner wear dress rings often?
- Are there any shapes, flowers or organic themes in their existing jewellery?

Once you have collated the answers to set questions like these, you will find that it helps focus your client's mind. Subsequently, it will give them confidence in your recommendations, which are based on the answers they provided.

The Google Image Search – Visit Images.google.com

When a customer is unsure of what they want, I ask them to search on Google Images. Sometimes, I do this in store with them. Nine times out of ten, this is highly inspirational and it helps guide the customer towards an agreed design brief.

By simply typing in a description of the item your customer is wanting, a huge database of similar or related designs come up. This brings on a rush of ideas and inspiring elements, based on the results displayed.

"I like the way that setting curves out there," or, "that's how I would like the band to be."

The Pinterest Board – Visit www.pinterest.com

Another useful online tool is a Pinterest board. It literally is a mood board of images on a single page, sourced from pages across the web.

Try asking your customer to create a Pinterest board of styles and designs they find online. It will inspire the new custom design.

2. Collate

Before interacting with a 3D Modeller, it's important to ensure you have detailed information from your client on what type of product they want designed.

A jewellery designer will create a concept board for the creation of a jewellery collection. Similarly, you need to collate information, images and/or sketches with your client, so that everyone is on the same page when it comes to creating the product.

Custom design is often an amalgamation of inspiration taken from existing designs, in addition to the input from the customer. Using the answers and feedback given during the discovery stage, I recommend doing a Google Image search for inspiration, or search through your portfolio or database.

Show your client examples of different setting styles, the shape and size of existing pieces, the shape and size of gemstones that can be used, examples of different fittings/parts and examples of different metal alloys and their colours. If you can show physical examples of these, it will help increase the level of satisfaction of the final piece.

Start to collate a concept board of the inspirations your client seems to prefer. Use this to steer the client towards making an informed decision on the final product. It is important to ensure your client feels they are making the final decision with your guidance and expertise.

This concept board will be the base for the design submission in the next stage.

3. Draw
When first submitting your custom job to a 3D Modeller to draw, it is important to ensure that you have these key pieces of information ready:

- The Millimetre stone measurements for the key large stones in the design. Smaller stones sizes can be left for the designer to choose if unknown. These will usually be designed to fit around the key larger stones in the design. If you have a customer's stone, be sure to accurately measure the length, width and depth of the stone using digital callipers. This will ensure that the CAD design is created accurately, and the stone will fit perfectly into the design when it is set.

- The finger size required. When a 3D Modeller creates the 3D model, it is designed perfectly to a finger size. If the finger size is changed after the design is complete, the 3D Modeller will have to redraw the design, sometimes from scratch. They will most likely charge for this extra work. Save time and money in the 3D Modelling process by ensuring you have the finger size confirmed before submission.

- Following standard manufacturing guidelines when submitting your design will ensure a smooth fulfilment of your project. Many manufacturers will be able to provide you with guidelines for manufacturing tolerances. As a standard, Cadfolio ensures all 3D Modellers learn these tolerances before allowing them to start freelance work within the platform.

- Images or drawings of the design to be created in as much detail as possible. Ideally, you'd need four different perspectives. A 3D Modeller draws a jewellery design using four views: the top down view, the side view, through finger view, and a 3rd angle perspective view. If you can provide images for all these angles, the 3D Modeller will produce a more accurate and detailed design than if they only receive images from one angle.

I recommend using a numbering system to lay out the key details of the design you wish to create, with clear instructions and references to annotated images.

Here is an example design brief I would write to a freelancer:

1. Please design ring as shown in the images attached
2. Centre stone to be a round diamond, 5.01 x 5.03 x 3.21mm
3. Shoulders to be channel set with diamonds to 50%
4. Halo stones to match the size of the centre stone, so it looks like the image enclosed
5. Shank width to be 2.5mm
6. Shank depth to be 1.7mm at the back of ring
7. Ensure wires under centre stone crossover exactly as shown in image 1
8. UK size – M

Notice how clean and simple this list of instructions is. The 3D Modeller will have no trouble understanding what is required, and will comfortably proceed with the 3D model creation without any further questions.

You'll notice that I have not mentioned the millimetre size of the shoulder or halo stones in this design request. This was intentional as I was happy for the 3D Modeller to choose the size. If you are unsure what stone sizes to use, then the 3D Modeller will happily recommend sizes. This should only be done for small stones, however, which are to be supplied by the manufacturer. If larger stones have already been chosen, or the customer provides them, it is important that accurate length width and depth measurements are provided.

The biggest mistake I see jewellers make is the lack of key information and the use of unnecessary narratives in their request. The aim is to provide clear instructions that are quick and easy to read and follow. Once you start talking about where you sourced the stone from, or some other random information that is irrelevant to the 3D Modeller, problems start to occur.

4. Review

Once the first draft is received, it is important to review the design against your original instructions to ensure the 3D model has been created correctly. The clearer you can make the design instructions, the easier it will be to cross check.

If you feel the design fits the customer's requirements, then forward it to them with detailed pricing information. If the design is not quite right, I recommend requesting the changes with the 3D Modeller so it matches the customer's specifications.

Sometimes, the initial design created by the 3D Modeller will need some changes. The customer will have a mental picture of the design. The first draft is often close, but sometimes they will want some tweaks done to perfect it.

3D Modellers are experienced in making changes to existing models, and it is a common requirement. They will also be able to give feedback if a request is not achievable in the overall design.

Again, it is important to detail your alteration instructions clearly and concisely. Doing so will make it quicker for the

3D Modeller to process and deliver the updated version so you can present it to your customer.

5. Send

If you are satisfied with the design, then it's time to present the design images to your customer, together with the pricing information so they are ready to purchase the design that has been created.

Once they receive the design and pricing information, you should clearly outline the next steps, how to request changes and how to place an order.

A digital jeweller will let the customer fully interact with their design online from any internet-enabled device. The design should include prices for multiple metals, and the customer should be able to request changes via an online form without you having to be present.

If the customer is happy, they order the product online via the web link provided and the manufacturing process begins without you having to do anything. By automating the custom design process and the interactions with the customer, the time required to service a client is further reduced.

Clarity, efficiency and automation are the key elements of a successful custom design project. They should be present in all the work that is undertaken.

Custom Design Exercise

When working with 3D Modellers, it is important to have clear and concise design instructions, presented in a format they understand. Here are some exercises to help improve the quality of your design request information:

- Using a pair of digital callipers, practice measuring the length, width and depth of different gems, large and small. Compare your measurements with others
- Select a ring from stock and practice writing a clear design brief on it
- Work with a colleague to critique and improve each other's design brief
- Practice taking pictures of existing rings from the four CAD angles
- When submitting a genuine design brief, ask the 3D Modeller if any improvements could be made to your instructions

Notes

Manufacturing

Over the last decade, jewellery manufacturing has changed completely. Traditional mass manufacturing of fine jewellery is on the decline, with UK hallmarking figures showing a significant reduction in the quantity of pieces being hallmarked. This is largely due to the 2008 global recession, and the increased demand for lower value fashion jewellery.

Large Asian manufacturers are seeing a steady decline in volume orders, and greater demand for single piece custom orders. Small production runs that were once turned away by large manufacturers, now make up a large percentage of their revenue.

Automation and digital assembly is where manufacturing will see the greatest advances in the coming years. 3D Modelling and 3D printing are gradually changing the face of jewellery manufacturing, allowing for faster lead times, instant customisation and more efficient manufacturing process.

Digital design files can be easily shared across borders, facilitating the rise in digital design teams that span the world. A jeweller can now talk to a 3D Modeller in a different country, and receive a high quality 3D model that is ready for manufacture.

However, there are still many limitations in the manufacturing pipeline that restricts the traditional jeweller from taking advantage of this truly groundbreaking shift in manufacturing.

Digital files are just that, a file on a computer. Without the proper tools and processes, these files have no real benefit to a traditional jeweller. I still see jewellers emailing CAD files to manufacturers for quotation, which is a very inefficient process. It is often days before they receive a quote in return. Even then, it's a basic quote for a single metal and stone combination. The manufacturer then has to manually generate a quotation based on the elements in the digital file by inspecting the design.

A Digital Jeweller, however, doesn't handle any digital files and doesn't have to wait for pricing. Technology shared by the 3D Modeller, manufacturer and jeweller allows seamless interaction via a central system that pulls together all the data from the three parties involved. The system also provides each party with the relevant information they require to progress the job to the next stage as required.

The 3D Modeller can simply upload their design file to a central system. Automation then ensures the product is visually rendered and inspected on their behalf before it is sent to the jeweller.

The manufacturer's pricing data is already loaded into the central system. The jeweller can price and customise the digital design as they wish before placing their order. The manufacturer's 3D printing team receives the instructions directly, and the manufacturing process commences.

By automating the analysis of digital files, and plugging in their pricing data, manufacturers can eliminate any time spent on quotations. The technology does this for them.

Retailer or Manufacturer, What Are You?

In a bid to reduce costs when the recession hit, many traditional jewellers resorted to organising the manufacturing process themselves. They believe that, by buying the parts individually at a lower cost, they somehow benefitted from a lower cost of production.

This is one of the biggest mistakes a traditional jeweller can make. Drawn by the allure of bulk buying small diamonds and lower metal casting prices, what they fail to realise is that they are, in fact, reducing their profits and wasting their time as a result.

Parcels of stones are often uncalibrated, leaving the manufacturer to charge higher setting prices due to the assortment that must be done with the customer's stones. The order ends up being delayed due to non-fitting stones provided by the jeweller. This is frustrating for the customers, and it wastes the jeweller's and the manufacturer's time.

From experience, unless the retailer processes hundreds of custom made rings per month, and has their own casting facility, there is no benefit in trying to organise manufacturing themselves.

A digital jeweller embraces technology to automate much of the fine jewellery production. It should take no more than a few minutes to process an order with a supplier. In an ideal world, their point of sale solution would automate this, too. This then frees up more time to work on the value adding aspects of the business that drive sales and increase profits.

3D Printing

3D printing rose to popularity in the jewellery industry in the last 10 years, resulting in a gradual shift in the way fine jewellery manufacturing is organised.

Some would say that 3D Printing is already at the forefront of the jewellery industry. Although, I believe there is still a way to go until it is fully adopted as I feel that existing machines are still not quick enough for retailers to take advantage of this technology in store. The technology is still mainly used as a tool for manufacturers to produce parts for direct casting.

The latest Direct Light Processing (DLP) 3D printers can realise a physical ring made of resin in around 2-3 hours. If a machine could produce a piece within 2-3 minutes, in theory, a customer could select from a limitless number of digital styles in store and physically see them in person once they are 3D printed.

I am confident that, as technology improves, we will soon see desktop 3D printers that could produce 3D printed parts for customers to inspect in a matter of minutes, and cost under £1,000.

Manufacturing Exercise

If you find yourself organising manufacturing rather than selling your products, then it's time to automate this time-consuming process. The following exercise will help you identify suppliers that can automate pricing and production.

- Make a list of suppliers that offer a full-service solution for manufacturing products from digital files
- Send the top three a request to design a product from your specification, and ask for quotations to create the final product
- If you are unable to communicate with the supplier online, this suggests the supplier largely operates a manual process.
- Shortlist those that allow online interaction, automatic pricing and order management
- Place test orders to inspect quality and test reliability before making a choice of supplier

Notes

Summary

As you have seen, a digital inventory of products will enable your business to offer an ever-increasing number of products, whilst reducing the quantity of stock you require. By leveraging assets that you do not own, you protect your business from economic downturns. You can also be more creative with your curation and product offerings.

You are giving customers the experience of customising truly unique pieces of jewellery to match their budget, an experience which will encourage others to seek your products and services.

Custom design will no longer be a service your customers are unable to afford. Automated interactions with freelance 3D Modellers will ensure a streamlined design process, along with the low cost creation of new digital products.

Now that you have understood the power of a digital inventory and how it can transform your business, I'll share how you can present your business and its products in a way that attracts your ideal client both in store and online.

3. PRESENT

"People don't buy what you sell, they buy why you sell it."
Simon Sinek, Author of *Start with Why*

The way you present your products and services has a huge impact on your business. It is a key component when trying to differentiate yourself as a Digital Jeweller.

Everything and everyone that represents your business should have a common representation that is easily identifiable. Digital assets are now the currency of a forward-thinking business, and building high quality digital assets is paramount to your future success. No business today should be without a comprehensive and value adding website, one that allows consumers to discover more about you and the products you sell.

As a Digital Jeweller, you should have a suite of digital brand assets at your disposal, which your team can call upon to use in any marketing campaign. These would include brand guidelines, artwork and usage examples. Your brand should echo through your business, presenting a sign of quality, reliability and world class customer service.

Your Brand

It is essential to recognise that your brand plays an important role in your consumers' decision-making process. Your brand should resonate through all communications and advertising to present a consistent message to all your new and existing customers.

Simply put, your brand is your promise to your customer. It should tell them what they can expect from your products and services, and it should differentiate your offering from your competitors. Your brand should precisely project the type of jeweller you are, who you want to be and what you stand for.

Are you the lowest priced jeweller in your town? Or are you the most expensive? The most experienced? Or the most reliable? Is your product offering the most ethical, or does it provide the best value? You can't be all things to all people. What your business represents should be in line with what your customers want you to be, and nothing else.

The interesting thing about your brand is that it's never what you say it is. It is more what everyone else thinks of it. Therefore, the first place to begin when working on your brand is to find out what people think of your business, versus how you want it to be perceived.

By working on this one fact alone, you can begin to map out how you want your company to be positioned and seen by your target audience.

It all starts with why ...

Brand Values

At the very core of your business are its values. They are the centre from which everything radiates, and the real purpose behind the creation of your business. They are the reason you do what you do, and how you do it.

Having clearly defined brand values help create a clear sense of purpose and direction for your business going forward. It also helps your customers relate to your brand, which, in turn, grows loyalty.

It may be that your business has strong ethical sourcing policies or a fair trade policy that attracts a certain type of client. It may be that you have a keen eye for detail and quality, or you only sell the highest grade stones available on the market. Whatever your business stands for, it should resonate from your core brand values.

Brand Identity

Your brand identity is a collection of elements that are created to portray the right image to the consumer. Formally, this is presented in a brand guidelines document that is strictly followed by the company and its employees when creating content and communicating with the world.

Visual Identity

Your visual identity starts with your logo, which should create synergy across your website, your packaging and your promotional activity. Every form of communication with your customers should have your logo present. It acts as a symbol of your brand, and amplifies your values to the world wherever it is seen.

Colour palettes are also effective in reminding customers of your brand. If you decide to rebrand your business, choose company colours that you feel represent your brand, and include them in your logo design. A baby pink and white combination, for example, would represent a younger, more modern brand. Dark green and gold would make one think more of a traditional jewellery store.

By far, the best example of a jeweller with a strong visual identity is Tiffany & Co. The robin egg blue that adorns all its packaging and print material is known by millions worldwide. This simple but highly effective use of repeating the company colours through your business activities is a proven method for increasing awareness of your brand identity.

Voice Identity

Your voice identity is the tone of voice in which your brand represents itself. It also relates to the emotional core of your brand. It isn't what you say, it's the way you say it.

The style of your marketing material must convey your brand values through the way it is written and presented. Do you want to come across as personal and friendly, or formal and professional?

A personal tone in your marketing material would be written as if you were talking to a friend; in a more conversational style. A formal tone, on the other hand, would follow a very respectful and reserved manner, as if you were talking to someone you'd just met.

My recommendation for a digital jeweller would be to adopt a friendly, conversational style as today's society is more relaxed and comfortable with communication than it once was. Jewellery stores are becoming more welcoming as millennials now represent the majority of consumers, and they prefer friendlier environments to purchase from.

Brand Awareness

Excellent brand awareness is created by sending consistent messages, and the repetition of your values, out into the world. A prospective buyer, it is said, takes 7-8 touch points of interaction with your business, on average, before making a buying decision. Those 7-8 forms of interaction could be anywhere from social media, to print advertising and even your website.[7]

It is important to consistently send the right message to attract your ideal customer, and to broaden the reach of your message. Therefore, it is important to know your ideal customer so you can target them correctly, and not waste any advertising spend.

Super brands such as Apple, Nike and Google have grown their huge awareness by spreading their brand values and messages out into the world through everything they do.

---

7   https://www.mckinsey.com/business-functions/marketing-and-sales/our-insights/the-consumer-decision-journey

Brand Equity

Brand equity is your business' ability to add value to your products and services due to the perceived value your brand has in the marketplace. Brand equity is measured by customer loyalty, awareness and reputation.

Again, an example of brand equity would be Tiffany & Co, who can charge premium prices and have high margins on products that can be made for much less. By building their brand equity over time, consumers now hold their brand in very high regard. Consequently, they are happy to pay premium prices and keep returning for further purchases.

Only through constant attention to the brand strategy pillars mentioned above can you build your brand equity. By providing a consistent high quality service and product, you build reputation, customer loyalty and awareness. This, in turn, builds brand equity and allows you to consistently charge higher prices.

By having a clear brand strategy, you build brand equity over time.

Brand Exercise

Look at your existing reviews, speak to existing clients and even hold a focus group of your target customer to discover how your business is perceived.

Values
- Why does your business exist?
- What is its purpose? What is its why?

Identity
- How do people currently see your brand?
- How do you want people to see your brand in future?

Visual Identity
- What colours currently represent your business?
- Do you use a single font for all your marketing material?

Notes

Your Website

Your website should be treated as the main hub of your business activities and lead generation. It is no longer sufficient for a website to only provide information about your business and its opening times. Modern-day consumers expect more from their interaction with your business online.

Your entire product range should be online for your customers to browse at any time, along with clear indications of the delivery timescales for their potential orders. It should also include detailed information on the services you provide, and how prospective customers can take the next step in purchasing from you.

Below are the key elements your website should cover:

Curated Digital Products

Digital products should form the core of your business as a Digital Jeweller, so your website visitors can customise and personalise them to suit their taste and budget.

A curated collection is a group of products within a theme, such as nature inspired engagement rings or gifts for Valentine's day. You should be curating collections on a monthly basis at least, but ideally every week. Not only will it keep your website looking fresh with a regular new product focus, it will also give you a source of content to write about and share on social media.

Your website provider should be able to simplify the process of creating new collections of digital products with just a few clicks so that they are ready to view and order online immediately. The new products should be well presented with stunning visuals, and the consumer should be able to customise and personalise them immediately on your website.

Working with 3D Modellers, you'll be able to create new designs that are exclusive to you, as well as create unique collections of products that can only be found on your website.

By creating digital jewellery designs that are exclusive to you, you quickly differentiate yourself from other jewellers, whom you may see as competitors. With a totally unique product offering paired with a fully interactive website, you will be set-up and ready to thrive as a Digital Jeweller now and in the future.

Contact Information and Appointments

Your website should have an easy to find page with your contact information and opening hours as a minimum. Ideally, visitors can also book appointments and visually determine your exact location via a Google Map image on this page. They should also be able to interact with Google Maps for directions if required.

Visitors should be able to contact you easily using a simple form on your contact page, which will create a message in your multi-channel communication system. If you are not using a multi-channel communication system, then completion and submission of this form should generate an email to your inbox, from where you can respond to their enquiry.

Appointment availability should be clear to your visitors when they are booking an appointment with you. They should be able to choose from the dates and times shown as available. Using a live calendar link software, like calendly.com, enables a direct connection to your Google Calendar and is a great way to offer this functionality. Google Calendar is my recommended choice of cloud based calendars as it allows seamless integration with lots of software and is accessible from any mobile device.

If you don't have a live connection to your calendar, you have the option for an email to be sent to you with the appointment request, which you can then confirm back to your customer after you have manually added it to your calendar.

Independent Reviews

It is said that 88% of consumers trust online reviews[8] as much as personal recommendations, and 72% say positive reviews make them trust businesses more. By including reviews of your company on your website, the likelihood of purchases being made by visitors increases by 58%.

Independent reviews are essential on your website. It builds trust and convinces visitors to purchase from you. Place the reviews in at least three places on your website: your homepage, your product page and your shopping cart.

---

8 https://searchengineland.com/88-consumers-trust-online-reviews-much-personal-recommendations-195803

Independent review sites like trustpilot.com, feefo.com and yelp.com are all good examples of sites that have widgets you can integrate into your website, making your customer reviews visible to visitors.

Google Maps is often used to search for local businesses, so it's important that your Google reputation is up to scratch. As a starting point, I recommend requesting reviews using your Google business account. Visit mybusiness.google.com to edit your business location, and to get your business' unique identifier and review link.

About Us Page

Your About Us page is arguably the second most important page on your website, behind your homepage. It should be the page where you communicate directly with your target customers and build rapport with a short introduction into your business and its values.

Your About Us page should come across as genuine, passionate and caring towards your local community. It should clearly outline the purpose of your business and the reason you do what you do; the "why" behind your brand.

Commonly, this page includes pictures of your store, of your team and even short biographies of your team members to help build trust with visitors to your website. This is to ensure that you are not seen as a faceless brand. Also, visitors get a sense of the passionate team behind the scenes, and a perception of the person they can contact in case of any unlikely issues.

What other content could you add to your About Us page that would show your company in a more personal and welcoming way?

Support and FAQs

The modern-day consumer prefers to solve their own problems and answer their own questions. To "Google it" has become synonymous with being able to answer any question that requires an answer.

Your support centre should be able to provide answers to any questions your customers may have, and these should be searchable, similar to how they can search Google for answers on the web. Google will index your support articles. If, for example, someone searches for your returns policy with your company name, it should instantly appear on Google and link straight to your support article.

If you receive questions from a customer that are not covered in your support section, add it to your list of articles to write so that it's covered for the next person who asks the same question. The more articles you write to support your customers' questions, the more satisfied they will be and the fewer questions your staff will have to answer.

Frequently Asked Questions (FAQ) – should consist of the top 10-15 questions your customers ask on a regular basis. The answers you provide here should not be as detailed as the support articles. They should be quick to read and straight to the point. These common questions will generally relate to things like delivery times, your returns policy and your products, with links to further detailed answers in the support section. Positioning your FAQ list directly next to your support section will make it easier to find.

Mobile Responsive Design

Since October 2016, global websites were officially accessed by more mobile devices than desktop devices, and this trend is set to continue.[9] Ever since the smartphone was popularised by the Apple iPhone, consumers have had access to beautifully presented web pages directly on their mobile phones.

As such, it is very important that your website is easy to navigate on all devices, to ensure every visitor has a seamless and enjoyable experience. "Mobile first" web design is a term that is currently being used in the web development community to describe how websites need to be designed with mobile usage in mind first.

When selecting your website provider, be sure to check that the websites they offer are fully mobile responsive and easy to navigate on your mobile phone.

Website Chat

Website live chat software is a recent innovation that has soared over the last 10 years. It is now one of the more important features to include on your website. Live chat allows the browsing customer to ask instant questions about your products or services, just as they would do in your retail store.

---

9 http://gs.statcounter.com/press/mobile-and-tablet-internet-usage-exceeds-desktop-for-first-time-worldwide

There are many live chat systems that you can easily plug in to your website. I'd recommend choosing one that also interacts with your customer relationship management system. Doing so will ensure that all live chats with known customers and leads will be documented and can be reviewed by staff in future if required.

According to a live chat survey conducted by the American Marketing Association in 2016, customers who used live chat were three times more likely to purchase online.[10] This figure is not to be ignored. Live chat is now a feature expected by most consumers when browsing websites.

Payments and Multi Currency

The world is becoming an even smaller place, where consumers are discovering and buying an increasing range of products from different countries. You should now expect visitors to your website from all over the world. The more niche your product offering, the wider the reach of visitors who will come to your website.

To make it easier for foreign visitors to purchase your products, your website should offer the functionality to change the currency your products are priced in. To do this, you will need to work with a payment gateway that offers the ability to process payments in different currencies.

Stripe.com is one of the fastest growing payment systems

---

10 https://www.ama.org/Documents/how-b2b-marketers-leveraging-live-chat-increase-sales.pdf

worldwide. It's a payment gateway that I recommend you use for your ecommerce website. It's completely free of charge, with no monthly charges, and transfers payments directly into your bank account in as little as two days. It also facilitates payments in nearly all worldwide currencies, so you can offer your products in the visitor's local currency.

As a minimum, I'd recommend offering your products in the following currencies: British Pounds, US Dollars, Canadian Dollars, European Euros, Australian Dollars and New Zealand Dollars.

Website Exercise

Let's analyse the current state of your website to determine which elements from this section are missing.

- Can you add curated collections of digital products to your website?
- Do you have a contact page? Can visitors book appointments?
- Are you showing customer reviews on multiple pages?
- Do you have an About Us page, with detailed information?
- Can visitors find support information easily?
- Does your website work well on mobile devices?
- Do you have a live chat system allowing visitors to ask live questions?
- Can you sell your products in multiple currencies?

Notes

Face to Face

Many jewellery items are still considered emotional purchases, especially pieces with higher price tags, like bridal jewellery. As such, consumers still prefer face to face interactions with a professional, and to touch and feel the products they are looking to purchase.

Though, face to face interaction is declining in traditional bricks and mortar retail stores, we are seeing more office based showrooms being utilised as touch points to facilitate interaction with consumers.

As more consumers become accustomed to interacting with jewellery retailers in different environments, we will see demand for online virtual interactions with sales staff increase. So, it is important to know your ideal client, and what their expectations are.

Video calling functionality should also be considered for virtual meetings and order updates. It would be a great way to improve the service provided to long distance clients. Don't be afraid of trying something new. Ask for feedback from your clients regarding the interaction.

The Retail Store

Favoured by traditional jewellers, the bricks and mortar store has been under threat for many years now. The high street is no longer the thriving hub of activity and footfall it once was. Consumers are increasingly spending their money online, often comparing prices and discovering more about your business to help them make an informed decision on where to book an appointment or buy.

If you currently occupy a retail location, when a consumer performs a Google search for jewellers in that local area, it highlights information on your business. Your Google business profile should be loaded with useful information so that it stands apart from your competitors. The more information a consumer can discover, the higher your Google ranking in the list of potential matches, increasing your chances of receiving an enquiry over your local competitors.

Your business location, recent pictures of your store, Google reviews from existing customers and your opening times are the four key pieces of information that should be available on Google Maps. Also consider adding images of your team, the inside of your store and examples of the products you sell. You can even provide a full 360-degree view of the inside of your store to give the consumer a sense of what to expect when they visit. Download the Google "My Business" app to easily update the information shown about your business.

The look and feel of your store should be in harmony with your ideal client. An old, tired looking store with windows crammed full of old, second hand jewellery on vertical pads will attract people looking for cheap bargains and second hand jewellery.

A fresh-looking store, with well distributed products and a modern and clean sophisticated look will attract younger, more tech savvy consumers, who will appreciate the clean environment and relaxed atmosphere.

I strongly believe in matching the look and feel of your store with the type of consumer you wish to attract. A Digital Jeweller will usually target millennial and generation X customers, aged between 18 and 45. This consumer age group will have grown up with technology, and loves to experience new ways of interacting with brands and retailers. They expect fresh, inviting and unpressured retail environments that have transparent pricing both online and in store.

If you are a retail store owner, it's time to evaluate your store and the way you present your business. If you are to survive this digital revolution and become a true Digital Jeweller, be prepared to make big decisions and changes to how you operate your business.

If you currently occupy retail space and your footfall is in decline, weigh up the pros and cons of your current locations to determine whether you should relocate or renew your lease. Consumer purchasing habits are changing rapidly, and you should not expect your future to be safe, no matter how large your business.

Shopping malls are facing increasing vacancy rates as many retailers aren't renewing their leases due to the higher rent landlords are demanding, and increased business rates. Large enterprise customers are feeling the pinch, and store managers are under increasing pressure to reach sales targets despite footfall being in decline.

The true extent of the digital revolution is yet to unfold, so it is important to protect yourself against every eventuality.

The Showroom

With rising rents and business rates/taxes on commercial property, many jewellers are opting for showrooms instead, to help reduce overheads. Showrooms are private, appointment only locations where consumers can interact with your business representatives face to face. Appointments are booked in advance. For online focused jewellers, this is currently the method of choice.

Shared office space and meeting rooms are becoming more affordable. Even start-ups can set-up their offices at prestigious addresses, with well-presented receptions and meeting rooms.

Many shared office spaces offer no tie in contracts or up front deposits, offering you the most flexible set-up for your business. These shared spaces often have many locations where you can book meeting spaces within their network of offices at little extra cost. In theory, you could host appointments at different locations at different times of the week, thereby increasing the reach of your business across counties or states at little cost.

It is worth considering this set-up as an option, especially if you are just starting out. The flexibility it provides almost guarantees the opportunity to test the market with your product offering, and to make a profit very quickly.

The Virtual Meeting

The virtual meeting is increasing in popularity as mobile internet speeds increase. Mobile devices can now facilitate video calls between devices and browsers, from all corners of the globe.

Think about how you could leverage this technology to enhance your consumers' experience when they are unable to meet you directly. By organising meetings online with video conferencing software, you can still meet your customer "face to face" and discuss their requirements. It's almost as good as being with them in person. You can also share your screen to discuss potential design choices and explain your services in further detail.

Through providing the option of a virtual online meeting in place of a face to face meeting, your appointment software will book in virtual meetings automatically. The consumer can state their preferred method of communication during the booking.

Google Hangouts is a recommended virtual meeting software. It is completely free and very simple to use with your existing Google Calendar.

Visit hangouts.google.com to find out more information.

Take Appointments

By taking appointments online, you can manage your time and how you serve your consumers better, rather than waiting for consumers to walk in. Consumers can select specific dates and times that are shown as available on your automated booking system. By blocking out certain times each week for appointments only, you can measure the conversion rates of your appointments against the cost of generating leads. This is a very important measurement to monitor as it will help you calculate the cost of acquiring a new customer against the profit you make per customer.

My favourite appointment scheduling software is calendly. com, which allows you to embed their software with ease into your website. The software has a live connection into your shop calendar, so customers can select a convenient time for an appointment without having to ask your for availability.

Instant Pricing

Imagine a situation where you could cater for every customer request in store. Imagine you could show them the exact piece with the stone combination they desire, whilst showing them the actual design as a physical piece to inspect.

By using a combination of digital visualisation and examples of the styles, the customer will be sufficiently informed to make a purchase, whilst also being able to view a wider selection of styles to choose from.

Taking advantage of a digital inventory creates a huge number of product variables, and it would literally be impossible to stock them all. A three-stone ring could quite easily have 166,888 variables if each of the three stones had 24 gem choices, and if it was available in 12 different alloys. Add to this the choice of diamonds qualities and sizes, and the different combinations are near limitless.

Face to Face Exercise

Fine jewellery is an emotional purchase, and always will be. Considering this, your website and offline interactions should complement each other, with your online presence working to invite footfall to your offline locations. Use these exercises to improve the relationship between the two.

- Google search your business and analyse how your business is presented online
- Are the four key elements of your Google profile present?
- Does your website make it easy to find your offline locations?
- Are you actively inviting website visitors to book appointments?
- Test a Google Hangout with your colleagues, then try your first hangout with a customer

Notes

Samples and Examples

By stocking samples and examples of products in your store or showroom, you can invite customers to view the style of ring before customising and personalising it to their wishes on screen.

The customer's involvement in this process results in a hugely satisfied and excited customer. Consumers are more than happy to wait 2-3 weeks for the delivery of their order when it has been made just for them. It also becomes a talking point for them with friends and family.

Silver and CZ Samples

Rhodium plated silver rings set with CZ are usually the preferred choice for example stock. They are typically at a low price point, so a wider choice of styles can be offered with a small investment.

From my experience, consumers are often unaware that the silver CZ samples are not diamond products. However, the experience of seeing a variety of style choices is still preferred.

Making customers aware that you stock samples so they can physically see more styles, along with assuring them that you have examples of real gemstones and diamonds for them choose from, provides a clear understanding of your sales processes at the outset.

Real Setting, Simulated Centres

Sample stock of diamond set semi settings are set with a large simulated centre stones to simulate the finished product when it is set with a real diamond. Having a large simulated stone centre drastically reduces the cost of stocking the ring from thousands of pounds to a few hundred.

Real examples are a better choice if you have the budget for it. It gives the customer a much better representation of the final product they are considering for purchase. Although silver and CZ samples are a great simulation of the final product, only real examples will bring out the true beauty and brilliance of diamonds.

Stocking settings with simulated centre stones is recommended if you wish to sell the stock mount at some point in the future. This option also allows for you to adjust the finger size urgently. It can be done in a few days, if the customer is in urgent need.

3D Printing Examples On Demand

As 3D printing machines become faster, less costly and more accessible, I am confident that we will see machines capable of 3D printing example in a matter of minutes, with multi-colour resin to mimic the colour of metals and gemstones, direct from an online platform.

For now, we have the technology to 3D print chosen styles in a single colour resin in a few hours, ready for the customer to inspect and try on.

This works particularly well for custom designed rings, where the customer prefers to see a real life sample of the ring before its final production.

Diamond and Gemstone Examples

Rapnet first created an online database of diamonds in 1996, opening access to tens of thousands of certified diamonds. Many retailers have since taken advantage of this global market data by utilising the lists as a digital inventory of certified diamonds.

Blue Nile was the first major retailer to fully leverage this huge inventory of diamond data, providing low-cost diamond choices for consumers via the internet. With a significant investment of over $50 million, they cornered themselves as the leading low-cost engagement ring supplier in the US. Recent advances in diamond and gemstone imagery has also resulted in the availability of high definition diamond images online.

Jamesallen.com pioneered the first consumer facing website, offering full 360-degree diamond imagery, which was subsequently purchased by the Signet group in 2017.

It will not be long before we see a combined extendable database of diamonds and gemstones with full HD imagery. Consumers will be able to choose the exact stones and visualise them set into their product choice, adding yet another layer of digital inventory for you to utilise without having to stock a single stone.

Samples and Examples Exercise

Samples and examples are the most efficient way to reduce your high value stock without sacrificing the number of products you offer. Carry out the following exercises to improve your sample offering.

- Create a list of products that you currently stock, ones that could be replaced by samples or examples
- Create a list of digital products you could stock as samples to grow your product offering and physical range to show customers in person
- Identify suppliers that can provide low-cost resin samples of digital products on demand, with fast lead times
- Curate a collection of real diamonds, gemstones and metals to help the customers make an informed decision

Notes

Summary

The way you present your business online is as important as how you present it offline. Consumers are more likely to interact with your business digitally before seeing or setting foot in your store. They'll research you on Google, read your customer reviews and then decide whether to buy, all from their mobile phone.

Your online and physical presence must align and present your brand consistently, providing a remarkable impression to new and existing customers. This synergy across all channels puts consumers at ease and reinforces their confidence that they are dealing with a modern reputable brand.

4. PROMOTE

"Without promotion something terrible happens ...
Nothing!"
P. T. Barnum - Entertainer

It is commonly known that, to generate sales, you need customers. To get customers, you need to promote your business. What is not common knowledge, however, is how to leverage free and paid digital tools that supercharge your marketing activity, and broaden your reach to potential customers.

Targeted and consistent promotional activity is how digital jewellers stay ahead of their competition. It also ensures that a steady stream of customers come through their doors.

In this section, I'm going to cover the main promotional activities that, as a minimum, you will require in this digital economy. These activities will ensure your business is heard above the noise, so customers can find you.

Lead Generation

One of the most common questions I get is: "How do I get more customers?"

My response is always: "Before you can get more customers, you need more leads."

Generating leads and analysing the results is a key skill you must leverage as a Digital Jeweller. Whether it is you who masters this skill, or a team of skilled experts, digital advertising is a necessity.

The money you spend on advertising needs to be supported by measurable outcomes. Measurable outcomes include the number of people who saw your advert, visited your website and, subsequently, made a purchase.

Digital advertising is one of the best investments you could make. It would give you evidence-based insights into the quality of your advertising campaigns, while reporting on its effectiveness.

It is also important to differentiate between leads and existing customers. Selling to existing customers is easier than selling to new leads, which is why a two-prong approach is best when promoting your business. Many jewellers make the mistake of neglecting their existing clients, and have no process to follow up with them.

Landing Pages

Landing pages are single web pages created to capture information from prospective leads who clicked through to your website via some form of digital advertising. These pages are also designed to match the exact advertising keywords or phrases the visitor is searching for.

I usually use landing pages for free giveaways of ring sizers or discount coupons/vouchers. To get the most from your landing page campaign, offer something of value in return for the potential lead's contact information. This will ensure they are confident you will follow up by email or phone.

I once gave away over 5,000 finger sizing kits by using a landing page and driving traffic from a Facebook ad targeted at people who had recently become engaged. It generated a huge volume of leads. I was pleased with the results, until I found out that someone had shared the landing page URL on a free giveaway website! Consequently, only 20% of the people who requested a kit became my target audience for this engagement campaign. So, 4,000 of the finger sizers went out to people seeking free items because of someone sharing it on a free giveaway website.

It's easy to give away something for free, as the above lesson shows, you must limit the ability to share the landing page information to ensure quality leads are captured. I recommend small quantities and short campaigns to ensure the above never happens to you.

There are many software options that create landing pages. CRM software also offers the option to create landing pages. When deciding on software, be mindful of keeping your software choices to a minimum. The more you can do within a single software package, the easier it will be to manage.

Pop-ups

Pop-ups are small boxes that are programmed to appear on your website when the user browsing triggers some set rules. I usually set pop-ups to appear for new visitors or when visitors visit a particular page.

When the rule is triggered, a pop-up appears on the screen. The user then needs to make a decision before continuing to browse. They either accept the offer you have presented and enter their information, or decline and close the pop-up.

Pop-ups work particularly well to generate leads, especially when you give away a free coupon to new visitors to your website. This could be for a discount off their purchase, or for free shipping.

Be careful not to trigger too many pop-ups for a user, as they will find their experience of your website frustrating. They are also more likely to leave the site completely. Therefore, I recommend only running a single pop-up campaign at a time.

Funnels

A funnel is a term coined by marketers. It describes the journey people take through a predefined set of web pages to entice a desired result. By pushing them through a virtual funnel of web pages where they have to make decisions, it forces them to convert, or not.

A conversion could include inputting their email address, filling out a form, downloading a free guide, placing an order or purchasing an upgrade. The goal of a funnel is to get the user to act, for anything you can imagine.

A basic real life example of this would be how airports funnel you through duty-free shops straight after security, hoping you purchase duty-free goods. At the checkout, there are enticing snacks to encourage impulse buys. On exit, you find yourself amongst a circle of restaurants and shops to tempt you to spend even more money. The airport is literally pushing you through a funnel of purchasing decisions, forcing you to make the choice to convert or not.

Funnels should be additional to your core website, designed to generate leads and capture additional revenue, which might otherwise be lost. As a minimum, I recommend adding a funnel to your checkout process by offering upgrades in addition to their purchase.

Since offering an aftercare upgrade to fine jewellery customers during the checkout process, we steadily increased our monthly recurring revenue. This monthly revenue now pays for repairs of returned or damaged items, and also covers our insurance premiums and utility bills. Soon it will also cover the mortgage payment on our building, and then, hopefully, our payroll. How can you add a subscription model to your business by offering it as an upgrade during the checkout process?

Lead Generation Exercise

Attracting and nurturing leads is an important skill to master to ensure a steady flow of enquiries continue. The following exercises will help identify ways you can capture leads.

- Identify what software options are available, ones that can manage landing pages and pop-ups, either within your CRM or as a separate software
- Brainstorm a list of offers, giveaways or coupons that you could feature on a website pop-up or landing page to entice visitors to exchange their details for your offer
- Make a list of additional upgrades, offers or aftercare packages you could add to your checkout process to increase the revenue per transaction in a sales funnel

Notes

Social Media

The way people socialise has changed, a shift brought on by the rise of the internet and mobile devices. Look around you right now. You'll most likely see people staring at their mobile phones as if it were a window into another world. In a way, it is!

Their attention has been diverted from traditional media like printed newspapers and magazines, towards the fast moving and infinite supply of news, reviews and opinions shared between themselves and others online. This is what we all know as social media, and a few major platforms have captured the eyeballs of most the world's population. The sheer volume of social media users is staggering, and this will only increase as more people learn to communicate and socialise this way.

As a digital jeweller, seize the opportunity to leverage the most relevant social media platforms, where your target audience congregates, to ensure your business is seen regularly in their social feed. This is where your consumers' attention is today. It is where you must be seen and heard on a regular basis. Your aim is to create curiosity that drives traffic from these platforms to your website. In the process, ideally, you capture their information with your lead generation tactics so you can remarket to them free of charge now that they are on your email marketing list.

At the time of printing this book, the recommended social media platforms mentioned below are where you should have a regular presence. Be aware, however, that as time goes by, the preference for social media engagement will change. Follow the social appetite wherever it goes and, more importantly, grab your ideal customer's attention.

Facebook

Facebook is by far the largest social media platform in the world, boasting a user base of over 2.2 billion active users as of 2017.[11] It also claims to have, on average, over 35 minutes of attention per user per day, which is staggering.

Facebook is quite simply a necessity when it comes to promoting your business. There is also a lot of functionality within the platform that is completely free of charge. Even as a traditional jeweller, you should have created a dedicated Facebook business page by now. It is currently considered the standard way to represent and communicate digitally with the local community, and the world at large.

You can post updates about your business on your Facebook page. Building the number of followers ensures you can get your message across widely, and completely free of charge. I recommend posting updates at least once a day to keep your followers up to date with your business activity.

Be sure to make your updates engaging and relevant. Also include a photo or video that relates to your post. Providing insights into your business and its processes, along with examples of your daily activity and the pieces that are in production. Consumers love to see posts about

---

11 https://www.statista.com/statistics/264810/number-of-monthly-active-facebook-users-worldwide/

the jewellery design process. How it is made and repaired is something they rarely get to see. Think about the unique pieces of content you can share to keep your Facebook followers engaged.

Facebook is also seen as an ideal place to run pay-per-click (PPC) ads to your target audience, which I'll cover in the PPC section later in this chapter.

Instagram

Instagram is another platform that has recently grown to new heights. It is one of the top places to share product content and videos with your followers. Posts on this platform are restricted to your mobile device, so it has built a reputation for quality imagery and videos, with less advertising in a user's stream.

It's important to not spam your followers with too many product shots and sales promotions. Instead, use this as a channel to engage with followers and share insights into the working of your daily activity.

Instagram is better utilised to engage users as a brand, share insights into your brand, show staff wearing the jewellery, share how it is designed and show snippets of the new collections being launched. This is more effective than pushing your products onto people.

By opening your business to Instagram followers, your brand will become more relatable and personal. It will build trust and also create transparency, which are proven ways to generate business in our modern social society.

Twitter

Twitter is a giant when it comes to the volume of content shared. As a small business, though, it can be difficult to get your voice heard on this platform. According to internet live stats, on average, 6,000 tweets per second are posted on Twitter, which is a staggering 500 million per day.

To rise above the volume of tweets, I recommend posting at least three times a day to get your message heard. If you feel this is too much content for your business to create, concentrate on Facebook, Instagram and LinkedIn. These three platforms represent the top platforms to post on at the time of writing this book.

LinkedIn

LinkedIn is the number one platform dedicated to business professionals. On average, LinkedIn users are generally higher spenders than users of B2C platforms like Facebook and Instagram.

Create a company page on LinkedIn, as well as personal employee pages, to generate as many connections as possible to broaden your post's reach. Many jewellers generate good sales from LinkedIn through connecting with other business professionals and sharing stories about their custom designs and services.

I recommend posting daily on the company page. Encourage your employees to also regularly share images of gemstones, custom designs, new stock and general business activity to build interest and following to your brand.

Planning and Scheduling

At this point, you may feel a little overwhelmed by the volume of posts on social media I recommended. But fear not. You can stay on top of social media posts by planning and scheduling your posts in advance.

Scheduling tools such as Buffer.com, SocialSprout. com and Hootsuite.com allow you to plan and schedule posts well in advance of when you want them published. This ensures same subject posts are synchronised and published simultaneously across all social media channels.

This also ensures you meet your objective of sending out a consistent stream of value adding content and social media updates. You will want to engage your audience so they turn to your website to find out more about your brand, and make purchases.

Social Media - Exercise

Your social media profiles are crucial to your online business profile. The following exercises will help you determine whether you have the basic elements in place to ensure your message has a broad reach.

- If you have not done so already, create business profiles in the top social media platforms to represent your brand in those places
- If you are not proficient with technology, try working with a freelancer or someone who understands social media to help set these up
- Brainstorm content ideas that add value and engage your followers and potential customers
- Create a plan and schedule regular posts on the platforms you have chosen to work with

Notes

Content Marketing

Creating content that is focused on helping your ideal customers discover your business is a proven marketing tactic. If done correctly, it can drive a lot of free traffic to your website. This free marketing strategy, also known as "Content Marketing", may seem like a lot of work but, if planned correctly, it can be integrated seamlessly as part of your daily or weekly routine.

Google does a great job in finding the most relevant content and information for users. By providing answers to the questions users search for, your website will be ranked higher than others on Google, and more organic traffic will flood to your website.

A good example would be an article that talks about the best wedding venues in your local area, with the title "The best wedding venues in (insert your town name here)".

Concentrating on valuable information for your target audience will ensure that Google sends organic traffic to your page when users type in a matching search query. Your website ranking will increase with every click on this search result.

It is safe to assume that most people looking for the best wedding venues in your local area will also be engaged, and the majority will not have purchased their wedding rings yet. So, these organic visitors, the ones who clicked on the link to your article, will also see that you sell wedding rings. Offer them some free advice, and they will form a positive initial relationship with your company.

Writing content that is relevant to your target audience is an example of how you can leverage content to work in your favour. From my experience, involving your staff in content creation can also be a great way for them to learn more about similar businesses in your industry. It will give them additional knowledge to support recommendations to customers whilst in your store or showroom.

Content Pillars

Creating weekly or monthly content pillars is a good way to organise the writing of content, depending on the amount of content you want to create. These content pillars are topics that are pre-planned, and provide a clear indication of what to write next and when. This way, you can have multiple content writers, who will know what to write about next and when it is scheduled to be published.

An example content pillar for this month could be based on content related to local wedding venues, as mentioned in the previous example. From this content pillar example, you could plan further subtopic content, which your target audience could research before a purchase.

For example:

- The top golf club venues in Kent
- The best castle venues in Kent
- The lowest cost wedding venues in Kent
- The highest cost wedding venues in Kent
- The top 10 wedding venues in Kent

Once you have a content pillar to work from, it's easy

to start brainstorming titles for articles that your target audience will find useful when searching online.

This example is targeted at brides, but you can create content pillars to target any audience by starting with a top-level content pillar.

Start a Blog

A blog is one of the best places to host your content so that Google can find and display it in their search results. Most good website management systems come with a blog editor built in, so you could easily manage the articles you create. Content can be left in draft form and you can schedule a publish date.

By communicating directly to your target audience via your blog, you can answer commonly asked questions in more detail to address your customers' most pressing questions regarding your products and services.

When planning your articles in advance using a content pillar, you can schedule blog posts weeks, and even months, in advance. This will give you a steady stream of valuable content to post on your blog, on a regular basis.

Create Engaging Videos

Screens are becoming increasingly popular. In turn, the consumption of online videos will also grow proportionally over the coming years. Given this trend, it is important to include video as part of your content marketing strategy.

It is said that 45% of the population now watch more than

an hour of video online every day,[12] and mobile video viewing has increased 100% year on year. Forward-thinking businesses could leverage video to offer more transparent views of their brand, whilst engaging customers through the medium they most enjoy.

Videos are often perceived as being difficult to create, but Instagram is a great place to start. You could create some short product videos of the jewellery you have in store, then share it with your audience. The jewellery box reveal is a good example of how easily you could entertain your followers. By simply filming the opening of a ring box to reveal a stunning ring you have in store, you create anticipation, excitement and intrigue all at once. A good tip would be to make sure you mention the product code and price in your post, so potential buyers can quote this when they contact you about it.

Other examples of engaging video content you could create are:

- Introduction to your store and what makes you unique
- How your jewellery is made
- The four C's of diamond quality
- How a service you offer works
- Unique pieces you have created that are available for sale
- How to measure your finger size

For PPC marketing purposes, I recommend shorter videos that get the message across within 30 seconds. Also bear in mind that over 80% of Facebook users watch video with the sound off, so incorporate subtitles in your marketing videos so the viewer gets the message without having to turn on the sound.

---

12 https://www.wordstream.com/blog/ws/2017/03/08/video-marketing-statistics

Content Marketing Exercise

Creating value adding content is a proven strategy that helps build trust and attracts ideal clients. Use the following exercises to create a content strategy you can build on over time.

- Create a list of 10 high-level categories for which you could write content for. For example, engagements, weddings, gemstones etc.
- Under each of these high-level categories, create another 10 subcategories to write about. For instance, top 10 engagement ring styles, top 10 local wedding venues, the 12 birthstones by month etc.
- Plan a weekly content pillar every week. Ensure you create content at least four weeks in advance to ensure you send a consistent message to your followers
- Think about how you could add video to the content you have planned. And focus on topics that are best suited for video. Film some wedding venues or some gemstones, for instance

Notes

Email Marketing

Email marketing is a great way of promoting your products and services with existing customers. However, it is not ideal for communicating with cold leads that have no previous interaction with your business.

According to statista.com, spam emails accounted for over 59% off all email traffic worldwide in 2017.[13] So, it's not surprising that most emails from unknown senders go straight into the user's junk folder, unread.

Email open rates are not what they once were. With open rates of less than 30%, email is now a more effective communication tool for existing customers or warm/hot leads only, where the recipient is already aware of you and you have permission to email them. Spamming a list of people who have had no prior interaction with your business will only result in a poor campaign. Your email provider could also ban you for sending large volumes of spam emails.

It is more important these days to gently educate your customer, and allow for self-discovery, to slowly nurture customers through a planned sales pipeline so that they are pre-sold on your products.

Email Newsletters
Newsletters are a great way to remind your customers of your brand every month. It keeps them engaged with your new collections and products on a regular basis. A monthly newsletter is recommended for your existing

13 https://www.statista.com/statistics/420391/spam-email-traffic-share/

customers, usually sent just before or after the end of the month, in line with pay day.

That said, it's important to not fill your newsletter with products and promotions. Include any news or stories about customers or staff celebrations in your newsletter. If you are a multiple store retailer, I recommend that each store organises their own newsletters, tailored to their customers in the local community. This regular interaction will help strengthen their relationship with their customers.

As a benchmark, for every customer you have in your email list, you should be aiming to drive 50p every month in sales. This means that, if you have 10,000 subscribers to your email newsletter, you should be able to generate at least £5,000 of revenue from your list monthly.

By planning ahead, you can ensure your emails also coincide with traditional gift giving holidays and calendar events. This will act as a reminder of your products and services ahead of special occasions.

Email Automation and Sequencing

Automating the delivery of emails to your leads has been proven as an effective way of nurturing leads as you feed them valuable information over time. When leads enter their information in one of your lead generation forms, add their details to your email list to trigger the start of a sequence of emails related to the products they are interested in.

Tailor the type of emails to follow up with, based on which page they filled the form on. For example, if the person requested a free ring sizer from a wedding ring product page, add them to a wedding ring email sequence and provide them with valuable information related to wedding rings.

These types of automated follow up emails are called autoresponders. This functionality is offered in many software packages. Ideally, you would want this functionality built into your CRM software. This will facilitate the storage of all your data in one place, and make it easier to manage interactions.

Email Marketing - Exercise

Email is a powerful tool for nurturing leads and enticing existing customers to make further purchases. When set-up correctly, it has been proven to increase engagement and revenue. Use the following exercises to plan your email campaigns.

- Shortlist software solutions that allow you to create email newsletters and trigger sequences
- Create a monthly email newsletter consisting of special offers, newly curated collections and news about your business
- Make a list of your core product categories and create automated email sequences for them to help educate potential leads about those products

Notes

Pay-Per-Click Advertising

Pay-per-click advertising has grown in popularity with small businesses. The concept and its potential has also grown significantly since its inception in 2000. Placing ads online is now a simple process and it is a great way of reaching out to your ideal customers.

Unlike print advertising, where the return on investment cannot be accurately measured, with PPC advertising you have full visibility of the number of people who clicked on your ad and viewed your landing page in turn. You are also able to monitor which campaigns lead to sales and conversions, then use this information to further improve your advertising return.

There are two main platforms you should be working with on a monthly basis to drive traffic to your website, and to help generate sales.

Google AdWords

Google AdWords is an online advertising platform developed by Google. Here, you can pay to have brief advertising copy, product listings, and video content displayed within the Google ad network. It will also reach anyone who uses the Google search website.

When a consumer searches for a certain product, they go to Google and type a string of words in the search bar. The consumer will then review the search results with the intention of purchasing from businesses that offers that product online.

So, by paying for ads to be displayed, in line with users' search keywords, you can direct your advertisement to consumers showing an active interest in the products and services you offer.

Each time a consumer clicks on your ad, your account is charged a small amount, and they are directed to the web page you specify. Therefore, as the pay-per-click title suggests, you are effectively paying for every visitor who is redirected to your website via your displayed ad.

Types of Ads

Text ads are the main form of ad type offered by the AdWords platform. You can write three lines of brief advertising text to entice the browsing consumer to click on your ad and visit your website.

Your ad copy needs to stand out from the competition, with your products and services clearly conveyed to the potential consumer. As you have limited space, include any key differentiators, such as your store location and any recent awards, and avoid unnecessary words.

Image ads are also commonly used across the display network. They are banner images that appear on websites not owned by Google, sites that have allowed Google to place banners there. Image ads are a great way to instantly capture one's attention, and generally costs much less per click. It's a great way to keep your brand active in your ideal customer's mind while they're browsing the internet.

Video ads are generally shown on YouTube before the chosen video is played. Video ads, when done well, are highly effective in driving traffic and awareness to your brand, and securing lifelong fans.

One of my favourite jewellery industry video adverts is by JamesAllen.com

Search YouTube for:

How Do You Know If A Girl Loves Her Diamond Ring? | Presented by James Allen

This video embraces humour with relatable real life experiences. The content is well thought out and has accumulated more than 3.5 million views on YouTube alone, a great brand lift for the company.

Whilst I am not saying you should spend huge amounts on creating videos, this gives you a good idea of how many views a great video can get when the right idea is applied.

Targeting

There are many targeting options within the AdWords platform. Over the years, I have tested many different options to determine the best return on investment.

For all campaigns, I recommend you use exact match and broad modifier keyword match types to ensure your keywords remain relevant to the consumers' searching.

If you use broad matches for your keywords, you will end up paying for clicks that are not relevant to the person searching. A good example would be an ad using the keywords "wedding bands". As a broad match, your ad would come up when people search for "70's wedding bands" or "Reggae wedding bands". In this instance, your ad would have no relevance to the person's search. These keywords would also be used by people searching for bands to play at their wedding. So, it's imperative you select your keywords with care, to avoid wasting ad spend.

For jewellers with stores or showrooms, I recommend creating separate campaigns for each of your locations. Within the ad copy, specify the location so the browsing consumer can instantly relate to this information. It would then more likely entice them to click on the ad.

Keywords should cover niche targeted phrases, and collections should be created to satisfy that list of keywords. Broad keywords like "engagement rings" tend to have lower conversions due to the variety of people visiting your site for products you may not have, or they cannot find.

Let's use the following to illustrate what I mean: rather than use the generic keyword "engagement rings", make a list of subcategories for niche engagement rings and use them to determine keywords, for example, "trilogy engagement rings" or "rose gold pink sapphire rings".

Targeting highly specific groups of keywords, and ensuring users land on the relevant page for those products, ensures a high click through rate, lower cost per click and higher conversion rates due to potential consumers being directed to a page that precisely matches their search.

Audiences

The audiences feature allows you to segment groups of people based on their interests and browsing behaviour. This will help you specifically target your ads. Simply enter keywords and website URLs that describe your ideal customers. Google will then identify and add people to your audience, in line with your descriptions.

After creating personas for your ideal customers, dig deeper to determine which websites they visit and what they like. This puts you in a better position to use this information to target that person directly, further pinpointing your ads.

Retargeting

The retargeting feature allows you to advertise directly to people who visited your website, then went on to browse other websites. By retargeting them with ads, you can set your banners to show on any other website they visit. This can be an incredibly powerful feature of your advertising campaigns. It can literally seem like your ads are following the user across the internet, wherever they go.

Facebook/Instagram Ads

The key difference between Google ads and Facebook/ Instagram ads are the types of interactions consumers have with them, and the purchase state they are in. When users search on Google, they are already in shopping mode. They'll be looking for products and services and making comparisons online.

When users are browsing Facebook and Instagram, however, they are not actively shopping around, so the users' frame of mind is different. This means that your ad copy needs to generate more curiosity to entice them to click through to your website, and ultimately buy.

Types of Ads

For newcomers to Facebook advertising, an easy way to drive awareness to your Facebook page is to "boost" a post. The boost post functionality allows you to specify the amount of money you wish to spend, and who you wish to target. For first time Facebook advertisers on a budget, I recommend you target people within a 10 mile radius of your store or location to ensure your local community awareness is kept active.

- Domain ads are the most popular type of ads on Facebook and Instagram. These allow you to create a post with content, and send traffic to a web page related to your ad copy. Unique pieces of content in the form of a post, with imagery or video, capture the users' attention with the aim of hitting the call to action button on the post.

Always include images or video in your ad copy to trigger curiosity and enhance understanding of the product or service you are advertising. There are multiple choices of image/video ads that Facebook allows you to choose from. When advertising a collection of products, I find that a carousel ad, which shows multiple images as the user scrolls from left to right, is a great way to show multiple product types. When the desired product is clicked on, it links directly to the appropriate collection.

- Lead ads are a novel way of acquiring customer information directly from the Facebook platform, essentially eliminating the need for the user to enter their details. The ads are like domain ads that link to a website by offering to show images and video. Instead of a link, though, the user is directed to a submission form where they can enter their details within Facebook.

My experience with lead ads has been varied. For free giveaways, it can work very well, but when used to encourage appointment booking or scheduling sales calls, I often find that Facebook users are reluctant to submit their details. By submitting their contact details within Facebook, some users feel they are letting companies into their personal space, which they associate with being spammed.

- Offer ads are perfect for advertising a sale or discount voucher. By specifying the number of vouchers available, and the expiry date, Facebook automatically distributes as many as possible to your targeted users. Facebook then follows up with reminders to users who claimed the vouchers, reminding them of the expiry date. This maximises the effectiveness of the campaign.

Targeting

Facebook and Instagram targeting is the most comprehensive of any PPC advertising platform available on the market today. As an advertiser, you can target the most niche segments of the population and convey your message to them for minimal cost.

If your company specialises in making jewellery inspired by dragons and medieval motifs, you can target ads to people who like dragons or enjoy the television series "The Game of Thrones". The accuracy of targeting within the Facebook/Instagram ad platform is truly amazing.

Demographics and interests are integral to targeting selections.

The easiest form of targeting would be to target people who are engaged. Serve them with ads related to your bridal jewellery offering. I recommend you test this in your local area with location targeting first, as other competitors could also be using this strategy.

Location targeting is also a key component of your ad targeting strategy. For store owners, targeting people within a 10 mile radius of each store is a good strategy to keep your business active in your ideal clients' minds. Another proven strategy is to target people present within a mile radius of popular wedding fairs or events you have presence at. This is known as Geofencing. The ad should invite fair or event attendees to visit your stand or location. This reinforces awareness of your company and sends a message to people who are likely to have an interest in your offerings.

Audiences

One of the most powerful features of the Facebook ads platform is the ability to create audience segments based on the rules you set. By installing the Facebook pixel code on your website, you can track visitors to your website and target groups based on their behaviour.

For instance, you could create a segmented audience of visitors who viewed a certain collection of products. If they have not purchased anything within a 48-hour time frame, you could show ads related to that collection in their Facebook feed. With a product feed installed, you can even go as far as reminding the visitor of the exact products they viewed, and even offer a discount.

Lookalike audiences are another great way of reaching potential customers. Facebook automatically recommends people who are like your existing customers. Facebook also increases the chances of your ads reaching your ideal customer by searching for other Facebook users who demonstrate similar traits.

This is truly remarkable! Advanced Facebook algorithms can utilise every single piece of information provided by the user, and the history of their stream, to identify like-minded people. Thereby increasing the chances of those users buying your products.

Retargeting

The retargeting feature is a proven technique that continuously nurtures potential customers who visited your website. Used in conjunction with audiences, you can show specific ads to customers based on the page they viewed or the collections they showed an interest in.

We use this feature to remind customers who have purchased within the last five days that they can track the progress of their order online by visiting the link in the ad. This not only re-engages the existing customer, it also takes them back to the website, potentially tempting them to purchases relevant additional services like aftercare on their order confirmation page.

Funnels and PPC Ads

The best campaign I ever launched, and continue to use, is a short video showing the viewer how to mould their engagement ring at home so they don't have to worry about searching for a wedding ring to fit their engagement ring. They can have one designed to fit perfectly through sending the mould back to us.

The buyer pays £3.95 for postage, and we send them a kit that includes free return postage to send the mould back. This small charge covers the cost of the kit and the return postage. During the checkout process, we upsell the customer with the ability to VIP their custom design experience for just £29.95. On average, 25% of our customers buy the upgrade, resulting in an average revenue per customer of £11.44.

By adding this digital upsell to the purchase of the low-cost mould kit, we get paid to acquire the customer. This is the beauty of a sales funnel. When executed correctly, it eliminates the cost of advertising the product whilst leaving the customer delighted with their experience.

This mould is then used to design a perfectly matching wedding ring, which can be shown to the customer before an order is placed.

This low-cost solution has driven thousands of customers to our stores, and even allowed us to profit from our advertising campaign!

Use an Expert

Without proper expertise, it is easy to lose money on PPC advertising as an inexperienced user would not have the necessary knowledge to accurately target and set-up the campaign for the most impact. PPC management is a growing business. Teams of dedicated PPC professionals can be found online, with the promise of boosting your sales

Be careful when choosing a PPC professional, though. They are generally more experienced in promoting fixed priced products rather than customised fine jewellery, just like the website platforms discussed earlier in this book. It pays to have a PPC professional or team that has direct experience in promoting the products and services that you sell.

Failure to choose a company/freelancer with an understanding of promoting fine jewellery will only result in wasted advertising spend, and frustration.

Pay-Per-Click Exercise

Pay-per-click advertising should be at the heart of your paid advertising strategy to drive traffic into your business. Use the following exercises to plan your PPC campaigns and measure the outcomes.

- Identify the core product categories you wish to promote via PPC advertising
- Search for, and hire, part-time freelancers who are certified on Google and Facebook ad platforms. They will be up to date on the latest PPC trends
- Identify your monthly budget for PPC advertising; start small and grow organically as sales and traffic increase
- Ask your chosen PPC partner to provide weekly and monthly reports on your campaigns and the outcomes
- Set-up niche collections of digital products to act as landing pages for dedicated PPC campaigns

Notes

Summary

Digital advertising should form the core of your promotional activity as a Digital Jeweller. The expectation that consumers will buy from you because you are the local jeweller is no longer valid. If you are not using digital promotional activity in your business, then focus on setting this up now, before it's too late.

Promotion should be an ongoing activity that sits at the heart of your business model. This will amplify awareness of your products and services to the world. Social media has allowed everyone to shout about what they do, no matter how small or large they are. You just need to shout the loudest and be consistent.

By combining free and paid advertising, and using proven techniques, you can drive more traffic and build awareness of your business to more people. By capturing new leads, you can communicate with potential clients free of charge while nurturing the new relationship.

As a digital jeweller, you will be able to leverage the reach and scalability of digital technology to get your message heard by the right people at the right time.

your business. It's your new digital shop window, where your brand resonates out into the world.

Finally, promote your business consistently using proven digital tools. You will continue to receive a steady stream of inbound enquiries. Working with experts to analyse your promotional activity will help you monitor which campaigns are the most effective and, based on this, you can steadily improve your advertising return over time.

To succeed, you need to follow the four steps in the correct order. Skipping parts will only delay your path to success. Some of the concepts covered may seem difficult to understand at first, so go back and reread those sections for further clarity.

This book is designed to act as a resource and a guide. Refer to it on your journey to becoming a Digital Jeweller. Share your views and opinions with colleagues and discuss the benefits of applying the methodology to your business.

Keep Your Heritage, Ditch The Tradition

Jewellery retailers often have a long history of family ownership and expertise. It is the reason many traditional jewellers are still standing today. Customers who purchased from them 30 years ago, still visit them today. This is testament to the quality of service these jewellers provide.

A traditional jeweller is somewhat a stereotype. The word "traditional" implies that the jeweller follows the same processes and presentations they always have. In this

FOUR SIMPLE STEPS, WILL YOU SUCCEED?

Becoming a Digital Jeweller doesn't happen overnight. You first need to change your mind-set, and the way your business operates. Apply the four steps covered in this book to a high standard, and it will force you to make the bold decisions you need to secure the future of your business.

Only by committing to change will you start to see the positive results of your ongoing efforts. With some persistence and guidance, you will succeed.

Preparation is the key to success. It is, by far, the most important chapter in this book. By planning the changes you need to make, and plotting out a path to success, you will smoothen the journey to becoming a Digital Jeweller.

Producing a digital inventory of products increases the number of product variations you can offer, whilst reducing the value of stock you need to carry. Empower staff with the instant pricing tools they need to make a sale, no matter what the product or specification, and you'll instantly see an uplift in sales.

Present your business in a way that allows remarkable digital interactions with your products and services, and you'll soon find that your website becomes the centre of fast-changing world of technology and innovation, it is evident that standing still and continuing with tradition is a recipe for failure.

Heritage, on the other hand, is something a jeweller should celebrate and share with the world. A long family history of expertise, craftsmanship and quality service is enough in itself to build trust with new customers. In most cases, the business has been built on many years of customer recommendations.

If you're reading this book and you're not in a position to bring about change, gift the book to a key decision-maker. You'll be surprised at how receptive they are to forward-thinking ideas; they will thank you in return. Unless you lead the conversation and express your thoughts on the subject, it's likely you'll be in the same position years from now. It's time to step up and openly discuss the concerns you have with your colleagues and recommend a solution.

It's Easier Than You Think …

Traditional jewellers can often feel like they're stuck in the past. When people observe the jewellery industry in its entirety, it's easy to see why. Until recently, you may have never considered the use of technology in your business, thinking the jewellery industry was more creative and curative. But now, with the growth of the internet, it's important that you leverage the available technology to your advantage – it is much easier than you think.

It's understandable if you feel you're not tech savvy, and doubt your own technical abilities, but technology has matured. It is much more user friendly than it was.

Look at the Apple iPhone. It's probably the most advanced piece of technology in the world, but it's also one of the easiest to use. If you can use a smartphone, then you can use modern technology to streamline your business. You don't need to be an expert to succeed – you just need to work smarter. After all, you're not trying to create the next Google.

The digital techniques shared in this book have been tested and perfected. If you apply these proven methods to a high standard, you will reinvigorate your business. Software companies spend millions of dollars on making their systems easier to use by non-technical people. So, test them out and ask for a demo. You'll soon see how easy it is.

You already possess a unique set of skills and talents. You just need to apply them in a modern way. Buying a piece of jewellery is still as emotional for your customers as it was in the past. The difference is that now you must provide them with an online interactive experience to facilitate their purchase.

Take a leap of faith and adopt new digital techniques; you'll wonder why you didn't do it sooner. It will take a little time to learn the digital skills you need, but your business will thrive as a result.

It Costs Less Than You Think ...

People often complain that technology is too expensive. But, I wonder, "compared to what?" It was once reasonable to assume that installing new technology would devour your cash and time. But time and technology has moved on, and the cost of technology has dropped considerably.

Originally, software companies sold their software products as one-off purchases. They charged high fees for a one-off license, and costs would mount depending on the number of users, support requirements and duration of the license. If you had ten people in the office, you'd need to pay for a ten-person license, even if only two or three people were using the software at any one time. This has now changed, and a significant proportion of advanced technology is now even free.

Software is hosted in the cloud, and can be accessed from anywhere. All you need to access some of the most advanced technology is a small, monthly payment. Product support is available in the form of an online knowledge base, and there is also a chat facility where you can speak to someone if you need help. Most problems can be resolved in your own time, and you only pay for the product features you need. A further convenience is that, if you wish to stop using the product, you can stop paying as you're not tied in.

This pay-as-you-go innovation allows accessibility of the software, without the huge upfront investments you might later regret. You can take a small calculated risk, one you can measure and, if it doesn't work out, you can cancel your account as you're not contractually bound.

This small monthly investment will allow you to streamline your business and automate most of the manual processes you spend unnecessary time on. By spending your time mastering your chosen software, you will end up freeing up valuable time as a result. Time in results in time out, and there can only be a positive result.

Experience Freelance Expertise

The internet has brought a new workforce that was previously not accessible. Today, it's easy to work with talented CAD designers on the other side of the world, as well as with those in your home country.

Digital interactions have no boundaries. You can now leverage talented freelancers from around the world to help you in many areas of your business. I regularly employ freelancers and remote workers to take care of many time consuming tasks that would otherwise cost a fortune if done by a local workforce.

Need help adding products to your website? There's a freelancer for that. Need help creating a new Facebook campaign? There's a freelancer for that. Need help designing new print material or graphics for your business? There's a freelancer for that, too!

Freelancers can be employed on a per project basis, or on a regular hourly wage. Therefore, your business doesn't have to pay for their lunch hour, other breaks, or any taxes or liabilities associated with an employee. You can take them on, utilise their skills, then let them go when you wish, without having to worry about laws or legislations.

When recruiting freelancers, the concerns frequently aired revolve around managing them and getting what you pay for. Trust is an important element when working with freelancers. For the most part, freelancers are a hardworking, honest bunch of people. I've rarely had a bad experience with a freelancer; they genuinely want to do a good job.

Providing a clear brief on what you require for your project is an important element in ensuring there is a positive outcome to your experience. By including a detailed specification with an explanation of requirements, your expectations and timescales to work to, your project will stay on track and complete successfully.

Digital Jewellers use freelance jewellery designers to lower the cost of production. Similarly, you could leverage freelance designers to lower the cost of marketing. Hire young, tech savvy people, who would have grown up in a digital environment. They will help and guide you, and happily steer you in the right direction.

Where do you find these experienced freelancers? There are a few great websites that take the stress out of finding the freelance expertise you need.

Try Upwork.com (formerly oDesk and Elance). This is a very intuitive platform that's been around since 2003. They specialise in hourly projects, so you can try out a freelancer for a few hours to see if they can work with you. This is my personal favourite, and it's easy to automate payments to freelancers from my PayPal account.

Freelancer.com, is more recent, but it has the most registered freelancers, with over 7 million skilled people waiting for your project.

Freelancers post their skill set, along with the types of projects they want to work on, in their online profile. You, the employer, can post a job description and invitation to pitch for your work. You then review the applications, paying close attention to their work history and reviews, before you make your selection. Payments are held in escrow, giving you the peace of mind that your project will succeed within the parameters you set. With each of the platforms, you receive assistance on arbitration if you are not happy with the work.

Don't be put off if you have a bad experience with freelancers. There are a lot of good ones out there. If it doesn't work out, try again. Actively interview them as part of the job recruitment process. It will reassure you that you're recruiting someone with the expertise you need in the relevant area. Once you find a great freelancer, you can call on them time and time again, as and when required.

Manage Your Time

Traditional jewellers often feel burnt out, and can feel they have no time to spend on the methodology presented in this book. This is usually down to the fact they're trying to do everything themselves: organising the showroom, ordering new stock and manufacturing the orders themselves. Perhaps they had to let a staff member go, resulting in more work for themselves. They need to realise that by taking on more menial tasks, ones that could be outsourced or automated, will only create more work down the line.

You don't have enough time because you're focusing your energy in the wrong place. It's time to manage your time more effectively, and to stop trying to do everything yourself. You need to free up time to work on the business and make the changes required to become a Digital Jeweller.

Every journey starts with a first step, so what could you do today to give yourself more time in the day?

Don't Be A Lemming

It's easy to get stuck on the same path, content with following the same strategy you've always had. You may have even convinced yourself that, if other jewellers are doing the same thing, then it must be right. But, being the same as your competitors will only result in a smaller share of the pie for all.

Look around today, and you will still see manufacturers pushing the same jewellery designs they have been selling for the last 10 years, and retailers are still buying it. What does that say about the consumers' experience? A product you see in one store, will also be on sale in the store on the next street. It's depressing to see so many large multiple retailers selling the same jewellery brands, the same watches and the same fashion brands.

Today's thriving Digital Jewellers are the ones designing their own collections of fine jewellery, and curating more niche designers and unique brands for their stores. In future, we will see more individuals becoming designers, and more independent businesses crafting their own unique brands through digital design and customisation.

It's more important now, more than ever, to not follow the crowd. Instead, use technology to help curate a larger variety of styles for your customers to browse online. Help your existing customers discover new and exciting pieces of jewellery regularly, and you'll turn them into raving fans.

You Cannot Do It Alone

The jewellery industry has always been considered a very secretive and closed industry. If you are the only one struggling, it can seem like an isolated place. But, this could not be further from the truth. Consider reaching out and engaging others for their help and expertise. National associations and organisations are there to support you as a jeweller, and there are plenty of opportunities for you or your staff to attend training programs and events.

Network with like-minded and digitally forward jewellers in Facebook groups or forums. Engage the community with your thoughts and feelings, and ask for help whenever needed.

Don't try to fool yourself into thinking you can do it alone. Taking advantage of experienced and talented people will ensure you avoid the mistakes they made, and help you reach your goals quicker.

Results Follow Action

Jewellers often claim to have spent years in the industry, trying out new marketing ideas and trends, yet never seen any growth or results. From my perspective, they're not seeing results because they're using tired and dated business models, instead of applying themselves in a modern way.

To become a digital jeweller, you need to adjust your mindset, not just apply a few tactics and hope for the best. You need to fully commit to the idea of embracing technology and a digital inventory. Half-hearted attempts only result in half-hearted businesses.

It's easy to get caught up in technology and the associated process, and forget about the bigger picture. Keep your clearly defined goals and targets at the forefront, and try not to deter from the path. Print them out and stick them on your wall. Let your colleagues have visibility of your vision. If you're accountable for your actions, you'll find it easier to continue along your path to success.

Dismiss those feelings of worry and uncertainty and have confidence in the proven method. Are you ready to apply yourself?

There's no better time than right now.

Persistence Brings Reward

Embarking on these four steps may seem like more work for your already busy schedule. At the start, it will entail more work but, with a little persistence and dedication to implementing change in your business, the results will come.

If it were easy, everyone would be doing it. The fact is, it's not, and it will take some time to implement these methods to a high standard. But fear not, your dreams are on the horizon. It will just take a little patience and focus to reach them.

Once you start to see more traffic and increasing enquiries, you'll start to realise the rewards of your hard work. By steadily opening the tap and focusing on organic growth, you will further perfect your systems and processes over time, without adding to your workload.

Initial results will come from your marketing efforts and lead generation. For me, there's no greater satisfaction than seeing my ideal customers react to our Facebook posts; customers who are keen to find out more about our products and services.

You Can Do This

The traditional jeweller within you will try to convince you to continue doing what you are doing right now. Deep down, though, you know changes need to be made.

Don't fall into the trap of convincing yourself that your business model doesn't need to change. Look around you and read industry related news. Every time you hear of a jewellery store closing, remind yourself that they probably failed because they weren't open to modernisation. Their stubborn refusal to change, sticking to conventional methods and convincing themselves the future can only get better, most likely brought about their downfall.

Don't fall into the same trap. It's time to act; it's time to become a Digital Jeweller.

You'll feel uncomfortable, you'll feel out of your depth and you'll have days where you'll want to give up. This is completely normal. Transforming your business can be a stressful time, but it will also be very rewarding.

People get stuck when they can't see the path forward.

Imagine how it will feel to run an automated business, one you could leave to run and earn money, while you enjoy free time with your family. Imagine waking up every day and not having to worry about cash flow, or where the next sales are coming from. You could run your business from your mobile device, leaving your digital ecosystem to do the hard work for you.

Be Brave and Go Forth

If you're stuck, or nervous about making changes, it's most likely because you haven't prepared enough. You might be worried about making a bad decision, taking the wrong path or, perhaps, you're not sure where to start.

Start with the end in mind. What is your goal? Where do you want this journey to take you? What do you want your business to become? What do you want from life? With firm visions of your destination, you can plan out your path accordingly.

This book provides you with a proven framework for you to follow. Take the appropriate actions, measure the results and expand your comfort zone one step at a time.

There has never been a better time to become a Digital Jeweller, and the sooner you begin your journey, the faster you'll meet your goals.

I wish you every success.

ACKNOWLEDGEMENTS

I could not have written this book without the support and guidance from a number of people, whom I would now like to thank.

- Thank you to my wife, Grace, for supporting me on this journey and providing valuable feedback on the book's content. I would not have finished the book without your keen eye for my grammatical errors!

- Thank you to my parents, Bruce and Denise Edkins, for believing in me and spurring me on to complete the book. Your love and support throughout my career has helped me achieve my dreams.

- Thank you to my mentor, Daniel Priestley, for your brilliant advice and guidance through 2017/18. As a result of attending the Key Person of Influence accelerator programme, I have learnt many new skills and raised my profile in the jewellery industry.

  http://www.dent.global/thedigitaljeweller

- Thank you to my booksmith, Debbie Jenkins, for helping me complete and compile the book into the structure you now see. It was an absolute pleasure working with you, and it was exactly what I needed to get me over the finish line.

www.debbiejenkins.com

- Thank you to Spiffing Covers, for creating a beautiful book and for working to my deadlines. I look forward to working with you again on the next project.

www.spiffingcovers.com

- Finally, a huge thank you to the draft readers who kindly provided praise quotes; they are mentioned at the start of this book.

RESOURCES AND NEXT STEPS

Take the Scorecard

If you managed to read this book without taking the scorecard, then I highly recommend you do it now! It's very easy to complete and will provide valuable insight into your business.

The scorecard is a free tool that will benchmark your business against the Digital Jeweller Method, and give you a deeper understanding of its current strengths and weaknesses.

Visit www.thedigitaljeweller.com/scorecard

Listen to the Podcast

Here I discuss important topics of the day with other industry influencers. I also tackle issues jewellers face daily. Join in the debate and listen to what others have to say while you're on the move.

Visit www.thedigitaljeweller.com/podcast

Read the Articles

Through my blog, I share insights into my thoughts and feelings on how digital technology is changing the world as we know it. My blog is where I discuss a wider range of topics around business, entrepreneurship and technology as a whole.

Visit www.ryanedkins.com/blog

Join the Platform

Cadfolio is an industry specific platform that provides a simple framework through which to communicate with digital jewellery designers around the world.

It is a platform I founded for the purpose of becoming a Digital Jeweller and to automate the design and production of fine jewellery via trusted, reliable and highly regarded manufacturers.

Visit www.Cadfolio.com

Take a Training Programme

Our intense training programs are designed to accelerate your path to becoming a Digital Jeweller. You can start generating online enquiries and sales in just a few short weeks, and it is by far the quickest route.

You will be guided through the four steps of the Digital Jeweller Method, and come away with a comprehensive solution that is proven to generate results both online and in store.

Visit www.thedigitaljeweller.com/training

Join the Discussion

The Digital Jeweller Facebook Group
Visit www.facebook.com/groups/thedigitaljeweller

Follow Ryan on Social Media

YouTube
www.youtube.com/ryanedkins

LinkedIn
www.linkedin.com/in/ryanedk

Facebook
www.facebook.com/ryanedk

Twitter
https://twitter.com/ryanedkins

Instagram
@ryanedk

THE ETHICAL JEWELLER

As a fellow jeweller, I thought it appropriate to raise awareness for sustainability and responsibly sourced materials, diamonds and gemstones in this book.

Ethically sourced materials and gemstones are not just a short-term trend, but a growing force that will help towards a better and brighter future for us all.

By taking an ethical stance in your business, you can solidify the way your customers see your business, and help rid the world of poor practices that are damaging our environment and affecting our ecosystem.

To find out more on how you can take part in supporting a more ethical and sustainable future, visit the following organisations:

Fairtrade Gold
https://www.fairtrade.org.uk/Buying-Fairtrade/Gold

The Kimberley Process
https://www.kimberleyprocess.com

The Responsible Jewellery Council
https://www.responsiblejewellery.com

GLOSSARY

CAD – Computer aided design

CAM – Computer aided manufacturing

SKU – Stock keeping unit

KPI – Key performance indicator

KYC - Know your customer

PPC - Pay per click

URL - A website address

B2B - Business to business

B2C - Business to consumer

3DM - The industry standard Raw file type for 3D models.

STL - The 3D Print ready industry standard file type.

ROI - Return on investment

CRM - Customer relationship management

MCC - Multi channel communication

THE AUTHOR - RYAN EDKINS

Ryan found his passion for the jewellery industry at a young age. At just sixteen, he started an apprenticeship with his father, training to become a goldsmith, creating fine jewellery by hand. As the apprenticeship was coming to an end, CAD design and 3D printing was coming to the forefront of the jewellery industry. Ryan quickly realised that this new technology was going to change the way fine jewellery was made and sold.

In 2009, Ryan launched his first ecommerce website, which quickly generated multi-million pounds in revenue over five stores, in just three short years. By leveraging assets he did not own, and by following the exact method described in this book, he was able to grow quickly without funding due to the cash-positive business model.

It is during this time that he developed sophisticated technology to automate the pricing, visualisation and production of fine jewellery from digital files. It's this technology and his passion that fuels the growth of Cadfolio, the B2B design and fulfilment platform that supports Digital Jewellers around the world.

A now serial entrepreneur in the jewellery industry, Ryan is bringing transparency and change to a once closed industry, helping experienced businesses, as well as newcomers, navigate the ongoing digital revolution.

Today, Ryan is focused on helping jewellers grow through the uncertain economic climate, using proven methods to increase their sales and leads into their businesses. You can follow Ryan's progress via his social media channels and join him on his vision to transform this very traditional industry into a digital one.